WALKING TOWARDS
CORDELIA

A STORY OF BECOMING, ACCEPTING,
AND THE JOURNEY TO GET THERE.

ELEANOR ANNE DOTE

ELLIEGIRL PUBLICATIONS

Walking Towards Cordelia
by Eleanor Anne Dote

©2023, Eleanor Anne Dote & EllieGirl® Publications

Paperback ISBN: 978-0-578-72569-7
Hardcover ISBN: 978-0-578-26907-8

Library of Congress Cataloging-in-Publication Data is available upon request.

Scripture taken from the New King James Version. Copyright ©1982 by Thomas Nelson, Inc. Used by permission. All rights reserved.

All rights reserved. Printed in the United States of America. No part of this book may be used or reproduced in any form or by any means, electronic or mechanical, including photocopying and recording, or by any information storage and retrieval system, without written permission from the author, except for the inclusion of brief quotations in articles or reviews.

This is a work of creative nonfiction. The events are portrayed to the best of Ellie's memory. While all the stories in this book are true, some names and identifying details have been changed to protect the privacy of the people involved.

EllieGirl® is a trademark of Eleanor Anne Dote

Cover Design by Eleanor Anne Dote, EllieGirl®
Edited by Anna Stigen & Lauren Vierra

First Edition (Paperback & Kindle): December 2021
Second Edition: October 2023
Hardcover Edition: October 2023
Published by EllieGirl® Publications
Pasadena, California

www.pastorellie.com
www.elliegirlcreations.com

*Dedicated to
my three amazing children.

I hope my story will help inspire you to live into your truth.
I love you with all of my being.*

PROLOGUE

I paused at the doorway, my heart pounding, just long enough to catch my breath. I must have taken two or three trips around the block just to make sure I didn't recognize any of the cars in the neighborhood.

"Can I help you?," a man behind the counter asked as I stepped through the door into the lobby.

"Ye-ye-yes," I stammered, reaching into my wallet and pulling out cash to pay the entrance fee. "I'd like a locker, please."

In exchange for my information, the man shoved a key attached to a coiled rubber keyring and a towel through the slot at the bottom of a bulletproof window. A buzzer rang at the next door. I took a deep breath, pulled the handle, and stepped into an experience that would forever change my life.

It was a surreal feeling - when you grow up hearing from so many people that you "must be gay," or that "they're just waiting for me to come out," you begin to start wondering if there's any truth to it. And after years of just holding it in and hiding behind my faith, the moment of truth had arrived. I had never been with a man before, although I had wondered secretly for many years what it would be like to do so. Time after time, I confessed it to my accountability group at church under the guise of "struggling with lust." If they had only known. If anyone had known.

I looked around at the men standing in the locker area in various stages of dress, and quickly found my way to the locker number on the keyring, and began changing into the evening's uniform - a terry cloth bath towel wrapped around my waist and pair of flip flops.

As I reached up to close the door to my locker, the sparkle of my wedding band caught my attention. For a brief moment, my thoughts turned to my wife. I loved her, really, I did. She was beautiful - the mother of my children, and put up with so much from me. I knew that if I was going to go through with this, I'd have to keep it secret. This would devastate her. Nobody could ever know. I sighed, and, removing my ring and placing it with my belongings, I shut the door to the locker and pulled the coiled keyring up to my bicep like I had seen the other men do. There was no turning back now.

A few moments later, I began to take my first nervous steps through the maze of hallways that served as the entry to a number of private rooms, each complete with a bed. From behind closed doors, the sounds of man on man sex emanated over the blaring club music pulsing through the overhead speakers.

Another man passed me by in the hallway, eyeing my body from head to toe. A slight smile formed on his lips, and as we passed, I felt his hand brush up and grab my crotch. I gasped but shook my head. I wasn't ready. Not yet.

It took me about an hour to finally get somewhat comfortable to the point of when I was sitting in the dark steam room, and I felt a hand reach out to touch me, that I gave in, allowed it, and reciprocated. His touch was gentle. My heart pounded and my breath caught in my chest as the reality of what was happening began to sink in, and I allowed myself to follow his lead as in the darkness his lips found mine.

I'm going to spare you most of the graphic detail here, but at one point in the evening, I remember looking at one of the men that I was with that evening and asking myself if I could see myself in a relationship with a man. The feeling of giving in to this compulsion was exhilarating and even pleasurable. But it wasn't me. I couldn't see myself attracted to any of these men - and there were some attractive ones there - as an emotional partner or lover. In this moment, I was just an object to be used. And I was okay with that.

I left that night, quickly and under the cover of darkness, trying to process the number of different feelings that were going through my mind. What did it all mean? Do gay men feel the same way? They only like men for the sex, but when it comes to an actual relationship beyond that - it was too much to expect? "No, that couldn't be it," I told myself. "Perhaps I'm broken. Am I the only gay man who doesn't like men?"

I kept watching over the next few weeks, knowing that I needed to be aware of anything I could have picked up in the bathhouse. Nothing appeared, and the tension surrounding that began to dissipate as the routine of "normal life" began to cloud out the memory of my one night of indiscretion.

At the same time, I loved my wife. I loved being married. I loved being a parent. What was this all about? A midlife crisis? The only thing I knew for certain was that nobody could find out. Nobody could ever know. So on top of my confusion and frustration, I piled shame and guilt.

The doctors called it depression. I accepted the diagnosis with open arms - after all, it meant medication that would hide the pain. The next several years were a blur - a mishmash of moves, jobs, schools, and children making the transition from childhood to adolescence. Life moved quickly, and with it the different experiments the doctors would make as the depression continued its spiral to take over my life.

There were several explanations for the depression — the biggest and easiest one being that I had stopped going to church. The abuse and pain that I had suffered at the hands of church leadership earlier made it impossible to belong to a church community let alone trust them, and so I allowed myself to drift into a dull existence where I focused on working hard and being a father and husband. The years went by without incident, and I began to believe that this was all that there was to my life. I accepted it. That is, until everything changed and the sickness started.

CHAPTER ONE

    The late afternoon breeze blew against my grey knit maxi skirt and tunic-length burgundy tank top as I made the short walk down the street from my parent's house to the neighborhood elementary school. Reaching the edge of the kindergarten playground, I paused, staring through the same chain link fence that separated my own early childhood experience from the rest of the world thirty-eight years ago. Gone were the jungle gym and monkey bars over patches of compacted dirt, but out of the corner of my eye, the balance beam caught my eye. It's the only remaining piece of playground equipment from my own time in an otherwise changing world, at least as far as playgrounds go. I smiled to myself, reached into my purse to grab my phone for a photo, and continued to stare at through the fence as the sun started its journey towards dusk. This is where my story begins, though I didn't know it when I was a student here. Truth be told, I wouldn't know it for another 35 years.

"Hey, Kim - wait up!," I half yelled, half-giggled as I ran after my best friend on the kindergarten playground.

"Why?" She paused long enough to glance back at how far behind I was trailing, her blonde braided pigtails swinging over her shoulder and her gingham jumper flowing gracefully behind.

"Because I can't keep up!"

"Move faster, slowpoke!"

"Hey!"

We collapsed on a lush patch of grass under the shelter of the two pine trees at the back of the playground.

"Look at what I found!" she exclaimed, proudly displaying three fresh flowers from the yard in her outstretched hands.

"I want one!"

I can't really tell you how Kim and I hit it off, nor do I know much of what happened to her after she left our school that year. I also don't quite know how I ended up gravitating towards the one of the most white students in the class. I remember thinking she was perfect - every day her blond hair would be brushed and either in pigtails or straight back with a headband so that it fell perfectly just below her shoulders. In many ways, I longed to be like her - with the neverending collection of dresses that looked like they were pulled from the latest Holly

Hobbie catalog and long flowing hair down to her patent leather Mary Janes. But alas, as a boy in the world it wasn't going to happen. As far as Kindergarten went though, she and I were inseparable for much of that year - including that fateful day when we learned about male and female careers in the beauty industry.

When we arrived at school that day, the two adjoining kindergarten classrooms were divided into two sections: barber shop and beauty salon. Three chairs were set up under salon-style hair dryers, and a small table covered in white butcher paper was set up with bottles of clear lacquer play nail polish. On the other side of the room, a similar table was set up with cans of Barbasol and bladeless razors, along with a large supply of combs and spray bottles filled with water.

There was a sense of excitement in the air, as we ventured to look at and explore the options before us.

"Children!" said our teacher. "Come and sit for circle time!"

We hurried into our spots along the taped-off circle on the carpet while awaiting the instructions.

"Today is career day!" she said with the excitement that only a kindergarten teacher could muster. "Does anyone know what that means?"

Hands shot up all around the circle. "Ooh, ooh, ooh!" became the repeating chorus heard around the room.

"Yes, Jennifer?" she called out to one of the girls in the circle who, while attempting to stay in the same place on the carpet was bouncing up and down and waving her hands wildly in the air. Another minute and she very well could have exploded.

"It's the day when we get to paint our nails" came the excited reply.

"Well, that's part of it, yes. But today we're going to learn what people who work in salons and barber shops do for their jobs." The teacher paused as the room began to quiet down. And, after a brief conversation about careers and instructions for the morning's activity, we were released to explore the stations on our own.

"Hey, Darryl -- " I looked up. Kim was calling me from the nail polish station. "You gonna join me?"

I grinned, making my way against the flow of the other boys who were streaming towards the shaving station, oblivious to the discrepancy between my gender and the side I was choosing. "Sure!"

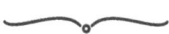

A passing car broke me from the memory I had been reliving. It was getting dark; time to head back home. I took one more reminiscent glance at the schoolyard and started walking down the familiar path towards home.

I guess it should have been evident to me back then. Perhaps it was, I don't know. In the days to follow, however, I would learn for the first time that my friendship with Kim and my decisions on that day wasn't part of the social norm. For the first time, I felt shame for what was my natural inclination as my parents and I were called to a parent-teacher conference after kindergarten let out for the day.

"We have no doubt that Darryl is a bright student," the teacher started. "But we have a few concerns that we wanted to share with you, Mr. and Mrs. Dote."

Those were the words that no parent wants to hear - and in kindergarten, no less.

"We're concerned because while he is socializing well, he isn't doing so with the boys of his age. He's made a friend in Kimberly, but spends his time chasing her around the playground and picking flowers rather than playing ball with the boys. "

I was shocked. Had I done something wrong? My parents sat in silence and to their credit simply thanked the teacher, stood up, and walked out the door with me in tow. But we never discussed the incident again and I was left to wonder if there was any reason why I should be ashamed about my choices in friends and experiences.

As much as I could say that this was an isolated incident, I'd be lying if I did. Each occurrence, while not involving my parents again, only served to push the natural inclinations that I had further back into the deep recesses of my psyche, as I searched desperately to find a way to hide it from the world. Thirty five years after my kindergarten experience would be the first time I began to unearth the identity that I had worked so hard to bury and never acknowledge.

In a way, I had unknowingly murdered the young, blossoming girl who only wanted to exist in the world as Ellie. Instead, I buried her spirit deep below the foundations of the house I would try to build and maintain until it was no longer possible to. But like the spirits in the movie Poltergeist, Ellie's spirit persevered, and as the cracks in the foundation began to form, the entire house came crashing down with a spectacular explosion. On top of the debris? A smiling, strong, confident woman named Ellie that had been screaming to be let out for so much of my life. All of my efforts - including hiding it all behind my marriage, my children, and religious ideology - weren't enough to keep Ellie a secret.

The skies had turned a deep shade of blue, and the silhouettes of the palm trees lining the backyard were the only thing I could see as I stared into the vastness of space. I looked down at my watch: six thirty. Time to make dinner.

"How did we get here, Ellie?" I wondered aloud. "How did we go from the conservative Christian and card-carrying Republican husband, father, brother, son, and church leader to here; a woman in transition?"

The silence -- apart from the background noise of the nearby freeways and chirping crickets -- was the only answer that would come.

CHAPTER TWO

"Before I formed you in the womb I knew you"
JEREMIAH 1:5, NKJV

There's not really a specific moment in my life when I can look back and think, "ah, this is where it all began." I wish there were, though I'm not sure why. Perhaps it's because there's a part of me that still looks back and thinks, "Ellie, you should have known so many years ago." All the signs were there, I just needed a roadmap and approval. In many ways, I feel like I still do.

With dinner out of the way and the dishes left soaking, I sat to think more about the memories that had begun trickling in this afternoon at the playground fence. Memories like this one began to be awakened, reminding me that Ellie really had been there all along. This memory took me back to my tenth-grade year — a full fifteen years before the bathhouse experience — and while much of the night was rather ordinary, this was one of the pins that I had stuck in my own roadmap, marking a memory on the road to becoming the woman I am now— long brown hair tied up in a messy bun, wearing sweats and a white cami, and sipping on a glass of sangria while letting my life story pour out through my fingertips and onto the screen. If I only could have given a vision of the future to the 15-year-old boy I was then...

The bed was cozy and inviting as I sank into the forest green comforter that covered my bed. This particular afternoon, the wallpaper caught my attention. As a young boy, my parents had taken it upon themselves to decorate my room as parents do — based on the gender that corresponded with what the doctor proclaimed when I came out into the world.

Images of cartoon baseball players, soccer players, and basketball players stared blankly with strangely satisfied smiles on their faces.

"Why did they get to be so happy," I wondered, considering that sports made me miserable. I sat up, resting my feet on the royal blue shag carpeting, and began to think.

I don't know what compelled me, but a few weeks earlier, one of the neighbors had donated come hand-me-down clothes to our family as they had kids close to the same age as my sister and I. In the jumble of clothes, I found a cute one-piece bathing suit meant for my sister and snuck it out.

I let the silky fabric of the blue lycra linger in my hands as I contemplated what it would be like to.... No, I couldn't. My mind flashed to memories of the kids on the playground, pointing at me and calling me a sissy while I spent time doing flips on the monkey bars and round offs across the grass field with the girls. Their taunts of "you're gaaaay," echoed in the back of my mind, and I quickly used those memories to shove the suit back into the drawer and underneath a stack of jeans. After all, I had gotten so good at doing the same thing with my own feelings - what was just another day in my fantasy life, anyway, right?

I closed the drawer and stood up, walking to my bookcase, and running my fingers over the spines, carefully sorted by series and book size.... Past the collection of Baby-Sitters Club and Sweet Valley High books... and finally landing on Dawn by V.C. Andrews. The pages and binding were worn on this one, as it was (and probably still is) one of my favorite comfort books.

I didn't understand it at the time, but many of the things I enjoyed reading early on in life were books that allowed me to see the world through the eyes of a female protagonist. I loved reading about the emotions and feelings stirring within Dawn as she dealt with a new life, new loves, and even the hardships she encountered along the way. I guess it's not a surprise then, that my high school years would find me writing my own stories from the viewpoint of a female protagonist — named Ellie.

I settled back onto the bed, reading, with the soft melodies of the Carpenters wafting in the background. Losing myself in the world of Dawn Cutler, my mind began to drift once again to the suit that was hiding in the bottom drawer of my dresser. After all, it was just a suit, right? And nobody needed to know, right? I shut the book and sighed. Perhaps taking some time to write more would help me feel better.

For a while, I allowed myself to escape into the fictional world I had created of Cordelia, the small suburban town that Ellie called home named in honor of my favorite heroine, Anne Shirley of the Anne series of books. Writing about Ellie's high school friendships, long flowing hair, and the way she loved to twirl in her dresses in the local field until she fell over, dizzy, and exhausted all felt cathartic to me. Her world still revolved around the same internal conflicts I had — teenage exasperation at parents and homework, heartbreak over guys that would never notice her. Yet, despite the fact that her world was far from perfect, it was perfect for me.

"Kids!," my mother bellowed from the kitchen. I opened my eyes and looked around. Gone were the fields. Gone were the wildflowers. Gone was the... skirt?

"Dinner's ready!"

I sighed. Reality set back in, and I was jolted back to the world I had left behind. Nothing had changed.

After dinner, I retreated back to my room, where I closed the door and sat back in front of my computer, allowing the familiar tones to welcome me back as I switched it on. The warm glow of the massive CRT monitor flickered to life as I smiled back at the computer icon greeting me on my 1992 Macintosh Performa. I clicked over to the familiar AOL icon and began the sign-on process, a lengthy series of beeps and static that at the time was strangely comforting to so many of us that were on the cutting edge of technology for the time. Finally, the words I had been waiting for: "Welcome! You've got mail!"

I quickly scanned through the emails of the day, deleting the various notes promising wealth and inheritance. Nothing new for today. I closed my eyes and began retreating back into Ellie's world. The books I had scanned from the library on creative writing had suggested that I try hard to get in touch with the characters that I was developing in my writing. Looking over my shoulder, I clicked on the link to switch accounts, and opened up the special screenname I had created for Ellie.

Ding! The familiar chime signifying an instant message sounded from the computer's speakers.

"Hey there, cutie!," read the message. I didn't recognize the screen name.

"Um, hello?," I typed back. "Do I know you?"

"My name's Ethan. A/S/L?"

I cringed. I knew what that meant. He wanted to sext. He wanted to trade nude pics, photos that were most likely not of him. Is this what it meant to be a teenage girl? Is this what my friends were dealing with on a daily basis? I hated to think that. Not wanting to deal with it, I closed the window and logged off of AOL.

Turning off the computer, I crossed the room once again and laid on my bed, pulling out my worn copy of Dawn once again. The swimsuit would have to wait for another time.

CHAPTER THREE

I dug around in my backpack for a while until I found them. The bottle of Advil was buried, underneath the weight of the textbooks, crumpled binder paper, and the spiral-bound notebook for math class. Ostensibly, I kept the Advil on hand for headaches. I snuck the bottle under my desk, and popped the top of it off — ten pills.

"That should be enough, right?," I wondered. "After all, the directions say 'don't exceed 2 pills at a time'."

I scribbled a quick note on a piece of binder paper: "I'm sorry," folded it, and put it in my pocket, silently crying to myself.

I thought it would be different. Here I was, a new school, a new surrounding. Away from the teasing I had endured through my elementary and junior high years. I had thought attending a Catholic school would offer some respite from the teasing because of its emphasis on faith. Yet here I was, with the teasing ten times worse. So much so that most of my time there, I can't remember to this day. But this particular event remains. It wasn't always there. Part of me wishes I could just shove this memory back into the shadows with the other ones that remain locked away in the corners of my mind, collecting cobwebs and dust. But I wasn't so lucky.

The bell rang. I left Spanish class and headed to the water fountain, where I quickly downed all ten pills. And now, the waiting. There wasn't any turning back now. I turned away and began the walk to my next class: religion. Well, here goes.

Half an hour later I began to feel my body react. It started with dizziness, then stomach cramps. With their onset, I decided that I needed to be excused, and so I grabbed my books and backpack and headed downstairs to the nurse's office, where I told them that I was suffering from a stomachache and nausea, and that I needed to go home. "After all," I thought, "I didn't want to die here at school."

The nurse called my mother, speaking with her briefly before handing me the phone: "If it's just a stomachache, rest for a bit and then go back to class. I'm too busy today to get you."

Part of me is still embarrassed that I ever thought that ten ibuprofen pills would do me in. The other part just found myself even more frustrated with everything around me. How could I deal with life? It felt so lonely, trying to navigate my life without being able to connect to anyone. I loved my faith. It was beautiful, transcendent, and gave me a purpose. But it wasn't where my peers were. I loved reading, but the books I loved - V.C. Andrews, Sweet Valley High, and L.M. Montgomery - were far from the books that my peers were reading.

Several years earlier, I walked with my parents through the doors of the Anaheim Convention Center and into the arena for the closing liturgy of the Los Angeles Archdiocese's annual Religious Education Congress. It's a spectacular event, much more of a production than the weekly mass that we attended at our home parish in Long Beach. There was a full band with a small orchestra, and a massive choir. I was in awe. I never imagined that the church experience could be so beautiful. What made it even more fun was seeing my uncle as one of the musicians on the stage.

For the first time in my young life, I felt a sense that this could be a place to belong. I wasn't finding that at school - it was a constant struggle for me to hide the feminine behaviors that triggered the incessant teasing and name calling; reminders that I was different. That I didn't fit in with the other boys. I had my girl friends, but as the years went by, their own social status became jeopardized by their connection to me, and so I found an escape in books. In imaginary worlds where I prayed I could belong.

"Could this be?" I asked myself as I looked around the arena that day. Had I found a place where I could belong? After all, I had been playing the piano for years by that point, and already had a relative "in the business." I decided I'd try and find out.

The rousing choruses of the final song, combined with the energy of the 7,500 attendees echoed through the room with a deafening roar. I found myself able to feel and experience the mass like never before - and nobody cared that I was bouncing to the music and grinning from ear to ear - so was everyone else.

As the mobs of people began to file down from the stands and towards the exit, my family tried to make our way to the front of the stage where the musicians were.

"Hi, Greg," my mother greeted her brother who waved back with a smile. He had his long dark hair pulled back into a ponytail that caught briefly in his guitar strap as he went to pack it away.

"Hey, kids," he called back, waving to my sister and I. We waved back.

"Hey Greg, great job up there." A woman was making her way from the piano towards us with her arms outstretched towards my uncle for a hug. "Who are these little ones?" she asked, gesturing to us.

"These are my niece and nephew."

"Well it's wonderful to meet you! My name's Jeanne."

"Hi," I said shyly. "I'm Darryl." I reached out my hand to shake hers.

"Nice to meet you, Darryl!"

"Darryl plays the piano" interjected my uncle. I blushed.

"You do?"

I nodded.

"Well, I'll tell you what. I just got this back from the publisher," she said, reaching into her purse and pulling out a cassette tape. The white cover was printed with a blue rectangle and the silhouette of a single tree. Above it were the words *After the Rain: Music for the Solo Piano by Jeanne Cotter.* She extended it to me with a smile. "Hope you enjoy it!"

We left the arena not long after that to join my uncle for dinner before getting in the car for the 10 mile drive back home. I took the cassette to my room and popped it into the boombox sitting on my book case. The soothing sounds of the piano began to fill the room, and I began to dream about what it would be like to be up in that arena playing the piano.

"One day," I thought to myself. After all, it was safe. It wouldn't matter if I was feminine if I was a famous musician, right? I began to wonder if music ministry in the church could be the place where I found sanctuary from the teasing. And one day, I would show those classmates that teased me on the playground for not playing kickball - I'd have my own cassette tapes with my very own name on it.

Jeanne and I would become good friends over the years, and not long after our first meeting in the arena, her second album came out. A combined piano project with her brother Richard, called "Coming Home," it would be the lasting tribute to her brother who died of AIDS in 1992. During a concert that Christmas, Jeanne spoke through tears while seated behind the black Yamaha grand piano in the sanctuary of St. Monica's Church.

"It was devastating to watch Richie's life slowly drain from his body as the AIDS virus took its hold over his immune system. I watched him, proud of his strength as he died in his truth as a gay man," she said, trying to hold back the tears. "When he took his last breath, my mother cradled him in her arms, weeping."

She paused for a moment before playing the opening notes to her piano arrangement of What Child is This? "As I thought about it, this song holds within it so many meanings, and while I can't stop imagining my mother holding Richie's limp body in her arms, I also saw Michaelangelo's *Pieta*. This is for you, Richie."

There it was. While I knew that AIDS was a real fear in the world at the time, the connection in my teenage brain had yet to be made between being gay and having AIDS. But there it was, right in front of me. Being gay meant certain death. I sat there in the church, silently trying to strike a deal with God: "God, if I promise to serve you, would you help me to not be gay?"

It's not that I thought I was truly gay; but after hearing it so many times on the playground and knowing that my natural behaviors and tendencies were obviously different, the thought had crossed my mind if that's what it would end up being.

"I'm going to do this, God," I prayed as the strains of "Simple Gifts" on the piano began to echo through the gothic interior of the church. "I'm going to dedicate my life to you in service so that I won't be gay."

The funny thing with being up front in ministry is that it forces you to hide your struggles further inside. When you're up front, you can't struggle. You can only lead. It's something I learned to do early on in ministry. And the higher you go, the harder it becomes. I mean, sure, you have confession but there you are, expected to confess to the priests you serve with your most intimate issues? And as a high school student? Yeah, it didn't happen for me.

Instead, I just internalized it all, even at some level trying to busy myself to keep the thoughts and feelings at bay. There were, of course, times when the feminine behaviors surfaced, no matter how hard I tried to suppress them — and it was in those times that I once again found myself being teased about my apparent "gay nature," painfully reminding me that I needed to be more careful.

"What would happen if they found out about you?," I constantly wondered. "I mean, look at how important Ellen was — and what happened to her when they found out: they took her popular sitcom off of the air and she was blacklisted from Hollywood for years. You're a nobody. You have your whole life ahead of you. Is that really worth the risk?"

These questions and messages would haunt me throughout the majority of my life. I found myself increasingly withdrawing as the ability to suppress my femininity became increasingly difficult. The Internet saved me. Even though it was the early days, when Prodigy and AOL were popular, I found social connection in a faceless world where nobody cared if I acted like a girl. My desire to connect with people led me to connect with other fans of V.C. Andrews and my favorite TV show, Avonlea, where I began to explore the idea of fan fiction and creative writing on those message boards.

My first stories were submissions for the Avonlea fan club where I introduced the character of a young girl — Eleanor Anne — as she navigated teenage life in her small tree-lined suburban city of Cordelia, aptly named in honor of Anne Shirley of the Anne of Green Gables series. The majority of my juvenile writings have since disappeared, but the one remaining story I do have has allowed me to realize that Ellie was there all along. My writing became a coping mechanism; a way of allowing her to come to the surface and experience life through her eyes while in real life I was doing the exact opposite: I tried to walk without a swing in my hips, sit without crossing my legs, and speaking in a more restrained tone of voice. Writing about Ellie allowed me the opportunity to escape into her world in my imagination. As Ellie, I imagined having a best friend akin to Anne Shirley's Diana. I imagined my bosom friend and I spending summer days running through fields of flowers, riding bicycles through town and giggling over the latest book we were reading. Even now, this fantasy brings a wistful longing to my heart. The closest thing to it happened the year I transferred away from that school and spent my senior year at a public magnet school for the arts.

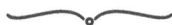

In the years to follow, I would find myself pining for that in a real-life experience; only catching glimpses of it through the lives of my gay friends — at a distance. Even into marriage and parenthood, I still often found myself wondering and wishing for the ability to fully experience the emotions and gracefulness that my female counterparts exhibited so freely. And yet, the only men who seemed to be able to do that were my gay friends. It was depressing, to be quite honest, especially since being gay was just something that didn't resonate with me, nor could I let it lest I suffer the same fate and shame that had made the AIDS victims one of the leading stories in the news.

CHAPTER FOUR

I threw myself into trying hard to drown out with church to overcome the struggle. By the time I was a sophomore in high school, I had made it up onto the stage at the Religious Education Congress playing the piano for the youth portion of the gathering. I began writing music, aspiring to be one of the composers and musicians I saw on a regular basis, and then my dream was realized as a piece I wrote with my friend Chris — a slow gospel song called Hunger No More — was one of the featured songs for communion. I listened as the crowd of 7,500 high school students clapped and sang along, and then the thunderous applause as it came to an end. I was so proud of myself - but it didn't matter. My identity crisis wasn't going away.

In the meantime, because I carpooled to school with another local student, I had begun to spend more and more time in the neighboring church's youth room after school, aptly named "The Upper Room." It was a fun and cozy hangout where several of the local youth came to hang out and socialize under the supervision of the youth leaders, Mark and Charlotte.

Earlier one morning, a dental appointment meant that I had missed the first half of my day at school. While in the waiting room, I had flipped through a copy of the teen Focus on the Family magazine for boys, "Breakaway," in which they had an ad for an upcoming national prayer rally called "See You At the Pole." It was a simple enough event - just a morning gathering where students would meet at the school's flagpole for a few moments of prayer before the day started.

"Prayer," I repeated to myself. "I know we're a Catholic school, but I'm sure that our school wouldn't be against prayer, right?"

I decided I'd go for it. I took the open magazine with me to the receptionist's desk.

"Can I help you?"

"Yes, um, I was wondering if you could make me a copy of this page? I'd like to take it back to my school with me."

"Sure, I can do that."

"Thank you."

After my appointment, I put the photocopied page into my notebook along with the note from the office excusing me for the morning. I went back to school, and after school, went to show Mark and Charlotte the flyer in their office.

"Do you think we could do this? I mean, it's prayer, right?'

"Well, that sounds like a great idea!"

"Awesome — I'll leave the flyer with you, then."

"Great."

The next morning, I was in the middle of my history class, when I got a note summoning me to the principal's office.

"I wonder what this could mean," I wondered to myself as I shoved my textbook and binder into my backpack and headed down the stairs.

When I got there, Fr. Nichols was seated behind his massive oak desk in his high-backed leather office chair - exactly what you would probably expect from the leadership of a private Catholic school. He was a formidable man, not very prone to smiling, and aged a bit. His hair was a silvery-white, almost matching the white collar that protruded from the black shirt. The uniform of the priesthood. On his desk sat a copy of the flyer — the one I had given to Mark the day before, but this time with the streak down the page that quickly identified it as having come from the Upper Room copier. He held up the flyer.

"Do you know who is to blame for this?" he asked.

His demand made me cower a bit in my chair. It was the first time the priests had ever confronted me like that. After all, I was the student on campus that was highly involved in my religious studies and was considered one of the main music ministers on the campus.

"I think so," I answered. "The copier —"

"I heard from a few students that you had this flyer yesterday on campus and that you copied it over at The Upper Room?"

"Well, I gave it to Mark to —"

"And you hung them up on campus without permission?"

I was shocked. I hadn't seen the flyer since I gave the original to Mark the day before.

"No, Father, I —"

"You were the last one seen with it."

"Yes, but I —"

"It's against the school rules to hang flyers up on the campus without clearance from the ASB office."

"Yes, but Father —"

"Besides, this isn't a Catholic event. It's a Protestant one. And we can't endorse a Protestant event at this school."

"Father, it's just pray—"

"I don't care what it is. You didn't get permission, and our staff has had to take down the flyers that were up all over campus. I'm giving you detention for the next three days."

"I —"

"I don't want to hear another word. You are dismissed."

Tears started to form in the corners of my eyes, and I gathered my belongings.

"Thank you, Father."

"Goodbye, son."

I went home and explained what happened that day to my mom, who called a meeting with Fr. Nichols. A similar argument ensued, and Fr. Nichols stood by his sentence. In a way, I have to say I am happy that happened though because looking back, it was the beginning of the end for my time at the all-boys school from hell.

On a side note, that same priest later confessed to the molesting of children decades earlier at a camp in Northern California. Despite the fact that he had this heinous crime from the 1960's and 1970's hanging over his head which he didn't confess until 2000, he still decided to unjustly accuse me of hanging flyers at the school for a prayer event.

CHAPTER FIVE

The three children laughed in their princess dresses as I watched on from the entrance to it's a small world. The ground was still slightly wet from an earlier rainstorm, and the children were delighted, splashing around in the puddles in their rainboots. They were oblivious to the rest of the world around them as they lost themselves in the joy of the moment.

It was an early morning, at Disneyland, and the line where I was working as a greeter was nearly empty. I basked in the children's joy.

My attention shifted to their two mothers, and then back to the children. Noticing that the child dressed as Rapunzel had short hair, I knelt down and asked playfully, "what happened to your hair, Rapunzel?"

The kid smiled at me, shrugged and then turned back to their friend.

"He just loves being a princess."

The comment caught off me guard. I stood up, fighting back the tears, and said "thank you. Thank you so much. He's beautiful."

"Yes, he is."

I don't quite know where the impulse came from to act "like a man." I suspect that it had something to do with what was reinforced in my life the deeper I got into the life of the church, coupled by so much of my life being filled with taunts about how "gay" I was. It was an impossible place, though — stuck between the conversations like these in which my peers would slap themselves on the back for "getting to the different bases" with the very girls that were my close friends at our sister school and youth group. Speaking out was out of the question because it meant even further ostracization and possible beatings. But these were my friends! My friends!

"I'll never be that type of man," I vowed to myself. "Never."

Wherever I learned about manhood, I remember feeling that it was at odds with who I was. I wasn't one to hold back my emotions easily. I preferred to be in the kitchen. I was the one who needed to be cuddled and told that everything would be okay. And yet, there was a shame in that. So I did whatever I thought I could do to be the "man" I was "supposed to be." It was exhausting.

And yet — there I was: a man, trying to live in this world as a father, husband, son, brother, and church leader. So many masks, and while I had convinced myself that it was who I really was, there was still a nagging voice within me that kept trying to get out. A voice that I tried as hard as I could to silence with church — after all, that was honorable, right?

Yet how often do we do that? From the moment we're born, we're taught to act a certain way. "Don't do that;" "that's naughty;." "smile more;" "cheer up;" "be a man." Where do those thoughts come from? Surely God has called us to experience more than the narrow range of emotions and behaviors that society has deemed "normal." Therein lies the conundrum that I spent 40 years of my life dealing with.

But what is "normal?" Here in Southern California, rainfall is considered abnormal, while in other parts of the world, sunshine and warm weather is a rarity. How much of our construct of the world is fashioned simply by what we know, causing everything that we don't understand out beyond the margins — to a place that we're uncomfortable with. And from there, we shut out the discomfort from our church doors. From our families. From our neighborhoods. And from our lives. We don't want to see them.

It's funny how much of that hasn't changed from the days of Jesus.

Story after story in the Bible shows us how those with disabilities or ailments were pushed out to the margins of the communities where they could be easily ignored. When Jesus began to spend time with those in the margins - loving them where they were — it made the religious people uncomfortable. So much so that they killed him.

We teach our children what our views of "normal" are, and perpetuate the cycle. Even now, how many years after the civil rights movement and Martin Luther King, Jr.'s "I Have a Dream" speech are we fighting for equality in communities of color? To emphasize that Black Lives Matter because we're seeing them die at the hands of those who were supposed to be protecting them? How often do we add to it by sharing stories of bad things happening, and making sure that we point out the thing that makes the person different? We long to distance ourselves from those things that we don't understand; yet in doing so we forget that we are limiting our ability to experience the fullness of all that God has to offer.

In early 2019, I experienced a powerful moment when a leadership cohort I was a part of ushered us into a room and invited to an introspective moment. Our intimate group of 50 LGBTQ+ Christians was asked to write one of two things on each of the three Post-Its that we were handed as we entered.

Our leader for the exercise was a beautiful young Black woman named Shae who had spent a good portion of our cohort teaching us about the experience of being Black in America and how racism and LGBTQ+ inclusion is inexplicably connected. "After all," she would say, "it's all based on structures of power and authority."

"For those of you who identify as white," she began, "I want you to write things that you think you can do to help break down racism in the world. Those of you who identify as a person of color are to write ways you experience racism in your own lives."

My mind went blank as I searched my memories to find something that I could write. Even as a Japanese-American, I grew up in a community that was primarily Asian, so I couldn't really come up with anything overtly racist that I had experienced. While I pondered what to write — which ended up being a few superficial things for me — I began to wander and see what my friends had started posting:

"I hate walking into a store and being followed like they're expecting me to commit a crime."

"It breaks my heart to know that if I or my future children get pulled over, there's a chance that any sudden movements or arguments might lead to them being beaten or even shot just because of the color of their skin."

"I manage a fast food restaurant and have had people ask to speak

to the manager. When they see me, they ask to see someone else simply because I'm Mexican."

"When I go to the store with my white friends, I'm the one that's always stopped at the door to show security my receipt."

The examples were heartbreaking, yet at the heart of each was one simple truth — when we fail to recognize God at work in those we don't understand, we allow fear to take over. How many times have you heard of a specific demographic - generations, races, sexual or gender orientations — spoken of in ways that raise fear or anxiety? The question I invite you to ponder is if it is from God or not. I'd venture to bet that more often than not, that fear is not of God.

So how do we solve this issue? Listen. Many of the things that my white friends had written involved simple things that didn't get to the heart of the matter. And yet, after reading through the pain experienced by the various minorities represented, it was a glaring indictment on how we could just learn so much more by allowing those without a voice to be heard. While the intentions were good, they failed to adequately provide a way for those who have been marginalized for so long to have a place at the table.

For much of my life, I learned by example that the things I struggled with - those internal qualities that made me different - were not safe. To share them out loud would be cause for alarm; a reason for me to be cast out of circles that I clung to so desperately because they were the only places I thought I belonged. The invitation to share and talk openly led to a shame and stigma that I tried to hide with activities and things in church that I fooled myself into thinking was "holy." If only someone had set the example to show that it was safe to talk… well, perhaps I could have saved myself the pain that was yet to come.

CHAPTER SIX

"Hi, are you new here?" came the female voice from the locker next to mine.

"Is it that obvious?" I laughed nervously, wondering what I could have done to give that impression.

It was the first day of my senior year of high school, and after a falling out with the priests at the Catholic school, my parents had finally relented and allowed me to audition as a pianist for a spot at the prestigious Orange County High School of the Arts, an after-school magnet program on the campus of a public high school in Los Alamitos. It was a dream come true, especially when the letter came in the mail proclaiming that I had been accepted. Little did I know the culture shock that awaited me as I went from a small all-boys private Catholic school of 3,000 to a co-ed public school where my entire senior class numbered

3,000. I had spent the majority of my day in a daze, trying to find my way around the sprawling campus and wondering where I would end up fitting in. The school day was finally over and I was trying to gather what I needed to take home with me.

The door to the locker next to mine swung shut, and I looked to see a tall girl with long orange hair straight down to her back standing next to me, hand outstretched. She was a curious one — unfazed by the latest fashion trends that so many of the popular kids were wearing, she wore a simple pair of jeans and a plaid button-down long-sleeve shirt. In many ways, it made me pause as I thought I was looking at a modern-day version of Anne Shirley from Green Gables.

I shook her hand and smiled. "I'm Darryl."

"Robin."

"Nice to meet you, Robin. And yes, it's my first day here."

"Well, if you want, I can be your friend."

"Sure, I'd like that."

"If you're waiting for a ride, you can wait with me - I sit up here with a group of art students."

She introduced me to Matt, a tall white boy with blond curly hair and blue eyes.

"Heather is usually here too, but -"

"Her mom already got her," interjected Matt.

"Ah. Well, you'll meet her soon enough."

We started chatting about my past, and I soon found out that both Robin and Matt were sophomores. In the middle of our conversation, we were joined by Robin's older and almost identical sister, Naomi, whom I would later find out was in my sixth period piano class.

A little while later, my mom pulled up, and I left the group after exchanging numbers.

"Oh, Darryl?" said Robin.

"Yes?" I asked, attempting the task of trying to stand while balancing my books.

"We eat lunch on the hill over there by the theatre," she said. "You're more than welcome to join us for lunch tomorrow."

"Sounds like a plan! Thank you!"

"See you tomorrow!"

I smiled. My first day ended with a sense of hope that the year was going to be okay.

The next day, I went and met Robin, Matt, and Naomi in the same spot, and noticed that Robin was reading.

"Whatcha reading?" I asked.

She responded by holding the book up - a worn copy of The Student Bible.

"Oh."

"Are you a Christian?" she asked back.

"Well, yes…" I answered. "I'm Catholic."

"I see." She paused. "Well, if you'd like, Matt, Naomi, and I are all a part of the Christian club here on campus, the 'Crossbearers.' We're meeting tomorrow morning out here before school to pray for the year and our campus."

"Oh! See You At The Pole?"

"Yes! Have you heard of it?"

"Yeah… it's a long story, but it's partially the reason why I'm here now."

"Well, you'll have to share that story sometime."

"But yeah, I'll be there tomorrow!"

"Awesome!"

My mom pulled up at the time in her forest green Chrysler LeBaron sedan, and I gathered my stuff, said goodbye, and started on the drive back home.

"Mom, do you think you can take me to school early tomorrow?

They're having a prayer rally before school begins."

"A prayer rally?" she paused, concentrating hard on the road ahead. "Yes, I think we can do that."

I smiled. I had friends. Friends who shared a similar faith to mine. And while I didn't know it at the moment, this was the year that was going to forever alter the course that my faith would take.

CHAPTER SEVEN

The next morning, I woke up early, threw on some clothes, went through the normal morning routine. I had no idea what to expect with this prayer rally - after all, at my previous school, the general consensus around prayer was that it was something that was only done if part of a class assignment or penance. Anything further was just superfluous. So imagine my surprise when my mom pulled into the school to find 200 students already gathered at the flagpole a whole hour before school was supposed to start. To pray. Not to pray for us to win that weekend's football game opener. Not to pray for good grades. But to genuinely pray for God's blessing over the school.

"What is this craziness?" I thought to myself. "We would never see a turnout like this at my last school for anything, let alone prayer. And this is a public school."

My mom slowed the car to a stop, and I quickly gathered my bags and got out of the car.

"I'll pick you up here after school!" she called.

I nodded.

"Have a good day, honey! God be with you!"

I closed the door and waved goodbye as she drove off and then went on the quest to find my friends. It was Robin who spotted me first and waved me over. I made my way towards her, noticing that many of the kids were holding Bibles. I got to Robin and was quickly joined by Naomi, Matt, and a few other people that Robin introduced me to — Mark, Jennifer, and Christine. Robin began to explain who I was and how we met when a short stocky boy called for everyone's attention. He introduced himself as Andy, the leader of the "Crossbearers" club and the ASB President. As he began to talk about how the morning's prayer was going to go, I started glancing around the group: a reporter roamed around the circle, taking photos as we prayed. We prayed, feet wet with the early morning dew of the grass, both in small groups of 3-4 students, as well as in a large circle, singing choruses that were unfamiliar, yet simple enough for me to pick up on the second or third time around. With a rousing chorus of Lord, I Lift Your Name on High, the rally was brought to a close and we disbanded to socialize for a bit before heading to class.

"Don't forget!" shouted Andy as the groups began to disperse. "We're meeting tomorrow at lunch in Mrs. Trujillo's room!"

"This is different," I thought to myself as I began the walk across campus towards my first-period class. "I've been in youth groups before, but the students here seem to really believe what they're saying. They're something more authentic about them and their faith, but I don't know what it is." The thought captivated my mind.

At lunchtime, I turned to Robin and asked them about the church they attended. They explained to me their belief in the Bible, which says that "all have sinned and fallen short of the glory of God." (Rom 3:23) I nodded my head in response — after all, that was a general part of what we did at Mass each week, wasn't it? They told me that when Jesus died on the cross, He did so for my sins - so that I could have a relationship with God. That God loves me, and if I would give my heart to Him, I would be invited into the most amazing relationship with the God who I had only envisioned as a distant concept in the Catholic church.

I was intrigued. For years, I had worked so hard to hide the feminine attributes that just came so naturally for me. The way I crossed my legs when I sat. The limp wrist when talking. The emotional squeals that came as a reaction to any exciting news. These were all things that brought on the endless rounds of assumptions about my own sexual identity, leading me to wonder what other steps I needed to take to avoid being gay. Perhaps this was it. A relationship with God.

The next day, at the Crossbearers meeting, Andy further expounded on our need for a relationship with God:

"You see, there's a giant chasm between you and God that can only be bridged by a relationship with Jesus Christ. There's nothing you can do on your own to be good enough. There's nothing to that will bridge that gap except for that relationship. You need to realize that you are a sinner — just like me — and that you need Jesus to come into your heart and life so that you can have the hope of Heaven."

I was floored. I had never heard God talked about in this way. Like a friend. The more and more I thought about it, I knew I needed this. And so when Andy gave the invitation at the end of the meeting to accept Jesus Christ as my personal Lord and Savior, I took it. I needed that. I had lived for too long just thinking that going to church and being active in church ministry meant I was good and going to heaven. But I still struggled with my feminine tendencies. "If anything," I thought to myself, "this doesn't conflict with my own faith as a Catholic Christian. I can still accept Jesus into my heart, have a personal relationship with God, and practice as a Catholic."

We were asked to stand — the three of us out of a packed room of 100 students — and repeat the simple prayer, asking Jesus into our hearts and asking forgiveness of our sins. We finished to a round of applause from our fellow schoolmates, and my new group of friends surrounded me, offering me hugs, and welcoming me into the "family of God."

"I'm so proud of you, Darryl" said Robin, giving me a hug.

"Thank you," I replied.

"If you ever want," spoke up Jen, "you're more than welcome to join me for church sometime — I go to Calvary Chapel in Seal Beach."

A new church? I didn't know what to think about that. I had worked hard to get to where I was in the Catholic church. That was my calling, I was sure of it. At that point, it was the only career path I knew. My heart was torn. What had I signed up for?

The bell rang, signaling the end of lunch, and we all departed for our different classrooms. I knew that I wanted to find a cure to this identity crisis — especially before it became an issue for me at this new school — but I didn't know how to do that, and I was counting on this newfound relationship with God to help me figure it out. But first, piano and music theory classes were awaiting.

CHAPTER EIGHT

My ears perked up at the words.

"Are you struggling with sin in your life?"

What did he just say?

"Is there something in your life that you've just been trying and trying to get rid of, but haven't been able to? Something that you KNOW God wants you to give up, and you've been battling it for so long."

I nodded, hanging on the pastor's every word. Here it was: the magic answer that I had been searching for all my life.

"Well, today we're going to talk about how to overcome the sin in your life."

It was a Sunday morning, and because I had the morning off from playing at my Catholic parish, I had agreed to join Jen for a morning at her church, Calvary Chapel Pacific Coast, which met in the auditorium of an elementary school in Seal Beach. The pastor, an older white man with white curly hair and matching goatee, he spoke and taught from the Bible like nobody I'd ever heard.

"I want you to take a look at this glass. Let's imagine that it represents you," he said, taking an ordinary glass and placing it in a shallow dishpan on a table in front of the podium. He then took a scoop of dirt from a bucket, saying, "this dirt represents sin."

From behind the podium, he grabbed two pitchers of water, saying, "now this water represents God. You see — if we have sin in our lives, we need —" and as he began to pour the water into the glass, said, "more of God in our lives."

I watched in awe as the water began flushing the dirt and sediment out of the glass. Two pitchers later, and most all of the dirt had flowed out of the cup.

"More of God in my life," I thought to myself, writing that down in the notes section of the trifold bulletin they handed me at the door when we entered. For the rest of the afternoon and into the next day, I pondered what that would mean, and how — if at all — it would affect my current position as music minister for my home parish and the Archdiocese of Los Angeles. I decided to research and find out what other

churches there were in my area that I could attend during the week. As it turned out, Calvary Chapel's original campus in Santa Ana had services almost every night, and various other Calvary churches had midweek Bible studies as well. I was set. I started out by going to a couple of midweek studies at different Calvary Chapels, then got involved with the college group at a local Reformed church. My attendance at the services increased, and pretty soon I was finding myself at church as much as seven days per week.

"More of God," I kept telling myself as I shuttled myself between school, work, and church services, listening to more Bible teaching and worship music in the car in each direction. And for a while, it seemed that my sudden obsession with Church and the Bible was actually doing the trick of keeping my thoughts from worrying about how my sexual identity was perceived — after all, within the church, it was "okay" for men to weep and feel emotions during worship. In addition, the church was also a place where people really didn't question sexual identity, especially if you carried a Bible and took copious notes during the studies. I started to tell myself that this was actually working. Of course, when school let out and I had more free time, I began to wonder if my faith was actually enough. "More of God," I said to myself, wondering what more I could do.

This cycle repeated over and over, each time pushing me further and further into the Evangelical church community. I left behind my promising career in Catholic music ministry and started pursuing my faith in a desperate effort to overcome who I was. In the coming years, I would enroll at Bible college, get married, start a family, become an associate pastor, and then work full-time ministry as a graphic designer at a church in the Bay Area.

The funny thing that happens when you think that you're trying to be more and more for the Church is that you lose focus, and what I had unwittingly done had allowed myself to swap "more of God" with "more of Church." So in 2008, the perfect storm destroyed it all when I left one abusive ministry situation only to find myself in an even worse situation at another. The stress and hecticness of this larger church ministry & Christian school left me without the time to deepen my own relationship with God. The constant amount of criticism left me cynical about church leadership, and by the end of the first year in my role, I was no longer attending church at all.

In its place, the thoughts and questions started edging their way back into my life. I no longer felt like I had to ignore the questions I had surrounding my own sexual identity, and yet I didn't know where I could turn. I found myself thinking about it and thinking about it until thoughts gave way to fantasizing, and wondering if the expectations were really true: was I gay?

"If I am, I definitely can't ask for advice from the church," I thought to myself as I began to try and strategize my next steps. Even though my faith had begun crumbling, I was still employed by them, and I couldn't risk anything that would risk my family's well being. We didn't have anyone outside of the church to turn to — our dependence was completely on the church.

It was during this time that the battle for gay marriage was in the headlines around California as Proposition 8 was on the ballot. The reaction that the LGBTQ+ community had towards people who were involved with groups and communities that were not accepting of them was scary as well, so the idea that I would seek out a local LGBTQ+ center to find support was out of the question. I was trapped with nowhere to turn, other than to hope for a way to escape.

CHAPTER NINE

The road was dry and dusty where the man sat, dirty and disheveled on the steps of the church. Here, he sat day in and day out, begging for money just to get by. As people shuffled in and out of the church, they were careful to step around him, ignoring his cries for help - some even going out of their way to exit another way just to avoid him.

"Please!," the man cried out as the congregants walked past him. Some, out of pity, dropped a few coins into his outstretched hand but did nothing to console or empathize with his pain, their superficial generosity only serving to ease their guilty conscience rather than help the man. "After all," they would tell themselves, "he must have done something to deserve this."

The man collapsed in agony, sobbing into his hands and wondering how in the world he got here. All alone. Abandoned. "There must be some reason," he thought to himself, "there's got to be a reason why I'm here. All alone. Unable to see."

The story isn't full of details, but one can only imagine that after the discovery that this man was blind, his parents - and his world - turned against him. No job. No healthcare. No help except the crumbs - the pennies - tossed to him as people hurried out of the doors of the church and on about their daily lives. Now, at 30 years old, this man had begun to believe that he was born cursed. Born with this punishment hanging over his head. Born to be exiled. Born to die alone. Without hope.

"Why me?," the man sobbed, "what did I do to deserve this???"

"Yes," a voice asked from the darkness, "what did this man do to deserve this? Was it his parents? His grandparents?"

Realizing that he was the topic of this conversation, the man began to cower and back until he reached the temple wall and couldn't retreat anymore.

"Neither," came another voice, speaking with a sense of authority that caught the man off guard. "There's nobody to blame. There's nothing to point to. Sometimes these things happen - but God, through everything, can bring glory and healing in its midst if you know how to look. Watch. I'll show you what I mean."

With that, the man felt a warm and soft compound being rubbed onto his eyes, with the instruction given, "go and wash this off in the pool of Siloam."

Now, normally the man would question what was going on, but the voice spoke with such authority that he left, searching in the darkness for the pool, and, upon finding and washing in it, he opened his eyes to see for the first time.

It was the summer of 2013, and I had been hired by a local water park to play the part of DJ and emcee for their weekend fireworks shows. In exchange, our family was given credit that we were able to use in the park for food and snacks on top of admission for ourselves and our friend. It was a welcome respite for us from the summer heat that much of California's Central Valley is known for.

Anyone who has been to a water park understands why it didn't completely surprise me when I began to battle various MRSA infections after a few visits to the park, along with a scalp that began peeling and flaking with what would later become severe dermatitis. And since that's probably not that much of a surprise to you, it wasn't for me, either.

Regular visits to the doctor led to a regiment of antibiotics and ointments, none of which helped. The sores began to persist and become more frequent. I began to battle with a few episodes of Bell's Palsy, an ailment that caused half of my face to become temporarily paralyzed. In fact, to this day I still have not recovered full functionality over the muscles in half of my face.

It was a constant struggle to remain conscious as time went on, and fatigue began to take over my body. Slowly, over three years and after several different medications that failed to work, my weight began to dwindle - until one day in the Fall of 2016, when I weighed in at 95 pounds and couldn't eat because of massive sores that had begun to form in my esophagus. Out of options as to what was causing everything, my doctor sent me to the lab for a round of blood work, and after taking several days off to rest, I tried to muster up the energy to head back to my full-time job as a web designer for a local design and IT firm.

I probably shouldn't have made the effort, as it was later that morning when I received the call. The type of call that everyone dreads. The call from the doctor's office. My labs had come back in.

"Hello?"

"Yes, Darryl? This is your doctor. I need you to come in right away."

"But, Doctor, I just got back into work after using up all of my sick pay - I really can't afford to leave right now. Can't you just tell me over the phone?"

"No, I'm sorry - but we need you here now." There was an urgency in his voice that I couldn't ignore. My heart sank, knowing that it wasn't going to be good news.

The next hour was a blur as I informed my boss that I was going to need to go to the doctor. I gathered my phone and keys and walked out to my car to begin the mile-long drive to the doctor's office. I can't say how long it really took me to get there, other than to say that time went in slow motion as I began to panic about dying - expecting that in a few moments I would be informed that I was dying of cancer.

I began to cry, thinking of my children growing up in a world without me. I began to worry about what still needed to be done at work and at home. The panic began to overtake me as I pulled into the parking lot and made my way up the stairs to my doctor's office. The receptionist greeted me as I stepped inside, checked me in, and before I knew it, I was sitting in the exam room waiting for the news that would forever change my life.

The room was abnormally cold that morning, and the protective paper on the exam table crinkled under me as I shifted my weight, nervously awaiting the doctor's arrival. After a few minutes, I couldn't sit still. I stood up and began pacing in the small room. A slight knock on the door, the handle turned, and the door opened. It was time.

The doctor stepped in, closing the door behind him. He peeled the stethoscope from the dark skin of his neck, almost as if he needed to rid himself of everything sterile in an effort to connect with me on a more personal level. I looked at him, trying to read his eyes for any sign of the reason for the urgency in his earlier call.

"Hey, Darryl - how are you feeling today?" His voice almost sounded nervous. Had he ever done this before — broken the bad news to a patient?

"I'm okay, I guess," I replied shakily. "Just wondering why you needed me here."

"Well, it might be best if you sat down for this," he said, motioning me back towards the table.

My heart sank. Here it was. The prognosis. I sat on the exam table, the white protective paper crinkling and loudly breaking the silence in the room as I adjusted to a place where I could be comfortable. Well, at least as comfortable as one can be when they're about to receive news like I was expecting.

"Well, Darryl, your lab work came back."

"And...?"

"And I'm sorry to have to tell you this, but you're HIV positive."

What I really heard was, "congratulations, Darryl - you don't have cancer!" A slight smile cracked over my face.

"Do you have any questions for me?," he asked after a moment.

I shook my head.

"Well, I'm going to step outside now and return with more lab orders."

I nodded.

The door opened and shut.

HIV positive. When did I...? How did I...? And then it hit me. Ten years earlier. That one fateful night. And it was then that I felt the blood drain from my face and my stomach fall. My past had finally caught up with me, and I had received the punishment for my sins. This was my death sentence, and I could no longer keep it hidden. This is what I deserved; after all, it was my fault, wasn't it?

I took my first steps out of the office that day knowing that everything to come from here would be different. I don't even remember making it to my car, but I do remember picking up my phone and dialing my wife, who was at a gathering on the other side of town.

"Hi, honey," she said.

"H-h-h-h-hi," I stammered.

"What's wrong?"

"I'm at the doctor's."

"Did they figure out what's wrong?"

"Well, um… yes."

"And…?"

The words caught in my throat for what felt like forever before I was able to finally get it out: "They said I'm HIV positive."

CHAPTER TEN

When I was growing up in the 80's, one of the things that scared me was the sense that if I was gay like the kids were saying, then chances were that I was going to end up getting AIDS and dying. As the diagnosis began to register with me, I was immediately reminded of that night in St. Monica's Church with Jeanne. If only I had listened; I knew the consequences. After all, according to some Christians, that's what God did to the gay community. It was Jerry Falwell who said, "AIDS is the wrath of a just God against homosexuals. To oppose it would be like an Israelite jumping in the Red Sea to save one of Pharaoh's charioteers. AIDS is not just God's punishment for homosexuals. It is God's punishment for the society that tolerates homosexuals."[1] I began to buy into it. This was my punishment - my fault. For a moment, the image of that fateful night moment when I removed my wedding band at the bathhouse flashed through my head. This is what I deserved.

The self-accusations began to roll in, and in rapid-fire succession:

"You cheated on your wife, Darryl."

"You should have known — this is what happens to sodomites."

"You didn't think you could get away with it, did you?"

Repeat.

There was no arguing that I didn't despise myself for that night. In many ways I still battle against that from time to time. The guilt of it swept over me like a continual incoming tide; wave after wave crashing over my head since the moment that the news came that I was HIV Positive. I prayed and prayed for God's forgiveness - reciting those well-known Bible verses that I had told so many other people during my years in ministry. Drifting in and out of consciousness, many of my waking moments became an internal argument with myself over whether or not God could forgive me if I wasn't forthcoming about how I really contracted the HIV virus.

I sank deeper and deeper into the oversized green armchair which sat perpendicular to the brown leather couch where my wife was sitting. I glanced her way as she watched another episode of Survivor on the TV. She sat in her normal position - lengthwise on the couch with her legs stretched out. Her brown shoulder-length hair was pulled back into a ponytail and our youngest daughter snuggled against her stomach and lap.

"Mom?" my daughter asked. "Is Dad going to die?"

I watched the tears start to well up in the corners of her blue eyes. The same eyes that I lost myself in those 16 years earlier that fateful night on Main Street USA at Disneyland.

"I don't know, honey," she said, squeezing her arms around my daughter. "I don't know."

By that point, the tears were starting to get to my own eyes. I wanted to blurt out the truth - that I had cheated on her. My wife. My beautiful wife Liz. The mother of my children. But thinking about the devastation that would follow — I couldn't do it. It was bad enough that the reality was we didn't know if she was going to become a widow or not. Maybe if I just kept silent and let my secret die with me, then nobody would have to know or feel shame about my sins. They would just be that - mine. I began to tell myself that if God didn't forgive me, that was my own fault. At least I would have saved my family the shame of knowing that I wasn't straight, not to mention a cheater.

Ding! My phone buzzed with a notification, jarring me from my thoughts. I grabbed at it, and with a few swipes saw that the first of my test results had come in.

"What is it, honey?"

"Hold on, I'm looking," I said, fumbling to navigate the medical app on my iPhone.

"Well...?"

"Um... it says that my CD4 count is at 26."

"Out of...?"

"I don't know!"

A few more clicks around, and I gasped.

"What?"

"It says that my viral load is at 422,888. I can't imagine that's good."

"Um, probably no — oh." This time it was her turn to gasp.

I watched the color drain from her face, and the tears began to fall. Speechless, she handed me her phone to show me: "A normal range for CD4 cells is about 500-1,500."

We exchanged phones, and as I read what she had shared with me, I shared with her what I had found on WebMD: "A high viral load is generally considered about 100,000 copies."

It was worse than we thought: a person that's HIV Positive is not considered an AIDS patient until their CD4 count reaches 200 or less. I was at 26. We looked at the calendar - the followup appointment with the doctor wasn't for another three weeks. Would I even live until then?

As we began to tell our close friends and family, the question that often came up was how I got it. In one of our first conversations, Liz asked me if I thought that I had contracted it when I had my oral surgery done eight months earlier.

"Maybe," I replied. It wasn't a complete lie, but I knew better. Yet the truth was harder, and I didn't have the strength to confront it all — not to mention the questions that it would inevitably raise.

We went with that as the explanation, keeping the focus constantly on making sure I didn't die. It was a task easier said than done, as each hour brought with it more exhaustion, and a fatigue which overtook my entire body. There were moments when I would fight it and lose — and as I felt myself fading I wondered if it would be the last time. I spent a month on the couch, thinking. Wondering. Asking if God could — and would — forgive me. I mean, I knew the answer. Everything in my Evangelical training told me that if I "confessed my sins, then He would be faithful and just to forgive me all of my sins and iniquities" — but that was the problem — I hadn't really confessed the sins that led me here to this place. And time was running out for me to confess. After all, this was my mess. I had created it, and I needed to own that.

So was this my punishment? Well, on one hand, I definitely wasn't innocent in the matter. I had engaged in risky behavior while cheating on my wife. I didn't use protection. But the question then lingered — was it an incident that called for me to face a lifetime with the HIV virus and the possibility of death? My Evangelical mindset began to believe so. As a pastor, we'd talk all the time about how we reap the consequences of our sin: teen pregnancies, drug addiction and homelessness.

How, though, do we reframe that conversation? What I'd suggest is to take a step back and see where the entire thing started. Author Glennon Doyle, in a recent interview for her book Untamed likened it to rescuing people from a river. "At some level," she said, "you need to stop pulling people out of the river and look upstream to how they're falling in to begin with." And that is the conversation I'm inviting us to have. It's a conversation that looks beyond the night I spent in the bathhouse to the mentalities that got me there — the inability I had to talk about my identity and the questions surrounding it before.

When we look at the atmosphere that much of the church has built for those in the LGBTQ+ community or struggling to come to terms with it, the question has to be asked how, then, do we anticipate that those who are trying to come to terms with their sexuality or gender identity are going to ever talk about it? Those that do finally take that brave step in many conservative Christian circles find themselves ostracized, humiliated, and referred to "therapy" in which they are mentally and emotionally tortured in an effort to "pray the gay away." For others, they try and suppress this instinct within themselves until they can get to a place where they're self-sufficient, then they risk everything, including relationships with family and friends to finally express their truth. The most disheartening part, though, is that a good number of them won't even get there — as statistics show that those who grow up dealing with LGBTQ+ identities in the church are 50% more likely to attempt suicide than those who do not grow up in the church.

Yes, mistakes were made. Bad ones. I had unprotected sex with strangers at a gay bath house. I didn't get tested after. Instead, I kept it hidden from everyone until I began dying and was diagnosed with AIDS. Yes, mistakes were made, and I own my part and my decision making in all of it.

Some might say that I had a choice. That the pain and internal frustration I was feeling was my cross to bear. That perhaps I should have prayed harder; been more honest in accountability groups; seek out somewhere to be honest about my struggles. Perhaps. In the meantime, how do you suggest that I do that and explore these issues privately as a father, husband, pastor, and church worker? Even whispering the words, "I think I might be gay; bisexual at best," could send my entire world crumbling to pieces — even at a time when I didn't even know. For those who are dealing with this issue in their lives, there is no safe space. Churches drive people like me towards self-hatred and suicide, and the LGBTQ+ community drive people like me towards a hatred of the church and God. Why is there not an in-between?

In our churches, people who struggle with an LGBTQ+ identity are dying. DYING. It would have been easy for me to be one of those statistics as well — in fact, there was more than one time when I honestly considered giving in to the disease in the nearly constant battles I fought against consciousness in late 2016. On more than one occasion the thought occurred to me that dying was probably going to save me and my family a lot more shame than having to live on with my regrets and the results of my sins. I knew I needed forgiveness. I knew I needed God. But here I was, asking the question of how a husband and father who was just coming to terms with admitting that he was bisexual and unsure if he was going to live into the next year could find a place to come before God and seek that forgiveness?

I shoved the thought far back into my head, reminding myself that the Bible said that nothing could ever separate me from the love of God, and that if I confessed my sins, He would be faithful and just to forgive me and cleanse me from all unrighteousness. I didn't need a church. Or did I?

As the thoughts began to float through my head one night in bed, I realized that the first step was going to need to be confession. I turned to my wife and took a deep breath.

"Honey, there's something I need to tell you…"

---

[1] 1993, quoted in Robert S. McElvaine (2009-04-07). *Grand Theft Jesus*. Random House. p. 35. ISBN 9780307395801.

CHAPTER ELEVEN

"You did WHAT?!?!?!??" she screamed.

I watched as the worry over my welfare in her eyes turned to hurt and anger. I didn't blame her. I couldn't.

"I… That week when I went back to the Bay Area to train my replacement?"

"Yes?"

"I went to the bathhouse."

"The bathhou— oh." Her words trailed off as she began to connect the dots.

"And that's where you…"

"Yes."

"Did you have sex with a man that night?"

"Um, not just one."

"Oh." She fell silent and collapsed onto the bed facing away from me.

"Honey, I —"

"Don't touch me." Her voice had grown cold and distant. "In fact, I think you should sleep on the couch tonight."

And so I did. I slept there for most of the week until a rowdy party in our neighborhood became an excuse for me to return to our bed, mostly out of her own fears of being alone in the room while the muffled sounds of the neighborhood drifted through the walls of our three-bedroom, two-bath house.

"So.... are you gay?" she asked, breaking the silence.

"No...."

"But you enjoyed it?"

"Well.... Yes, but I'm not attracted to men."

"So you're gay."

"No!"

"Then what *are* you?"

It was the elusive question. What was I? After all that - what was I? A typical straight guy doesn't have to figure out if he was gay or not by sleeping with other guys, right? But if I wasn't gay, then what was going on with me? What was different? Many of my friends from my younger years thought I was gay. I couldn't really be bisexual if I didn't like men, could I? And there we were - back at the bottom of an unending circle of questions regarding my own identity.

This circle of questioning would be my life in and out of consciousness as I began treatment and recovery from my close encounter with death. A regiment of medications was started, a variety of vaccines were given as an added layer of protection, and I resigned from my position at the local agency I was working for full time. I'd sit on the couch in the front room with the TV on to drown out questions in my head as I contemplated if it was going to be death or life for me.

"Ugh. Is there nothing on TV today?" I said to myself as I flipped through the entire menu of channels for the third time. "Wait — what's this?" HBO was playing *Philadelphia*.

For some reason, despite the fact that I knew that it was about a man who was dying of AIDS, I thought it might be beneficial for me to watch. After all, I never really knew anyone who had lived with this disease, despite the fact that we had all watched The Ryan White Story on the ABC Afterschool Special in the '80s. So I turned on Philadelphia and sat back with the intention of learning. Except that's not what happened. Halfway through the movie, I realized just what a mistake this was. I had forgotten that the accusations that began to fly against

Andy Beckett - how his struggle no longer became about his having AIDS, but that is was about him being gay. Cue the questions in my head. Again.

I wasn't wholly naive. I knew that the trans community was out there — but all I had seen from TV, the news, and the church was a strange world that I had no immediate connection with, either. Today, though, be it frustration or just plain curiosity, those questions that lingered on and repeated over and over again led me to the computer where I opened a new browser window to Google and found myself typing the words, "I'm not gay but I'm feminine" into the search bar.

"This will never amount to anything, but I need answers," I thought to myself.

My skepticism turned to surprise and then horror as I began to click through some of the results and related searches only to find one word repeatedly staring me in the face: transgender.

"No, that's not me," I prayed silently, as the tears rolled down my cheeks. "Please, Lord, don't let that be me." I could live with being bisexual, but transgender? That would change EVERY-THING, and at 40 years old, it wasn't really a risk I wanted to take. I was a father. I was a husband. I knew my place.

And yet, the more I read, the more it all began to make sense - the early years of trying to figure out why being with the boys just didn't feel "right." The pain and torture on the playground of being teased as "gay" or "faggot." The mannerisms that were seen by others to be feminine, and having to break myself of "bad habits," from the way I sat to the way I walked. I thought back to a time when I had to focus on walking without the natural swing in my hips because "boys don't walk like that." The more I read, the clearer it became.

I started searching for online quizzes to tell if I was transgender or not — as if a Cosmo quiz was going to be the all-knowing determiner of my identity. But I just wanted it to be wrong. But as bizarre as the quizzes were — a number of the questions had to do with math problems and not anything behavior-wise - and as much as I wanted them to prove this fear wrong, they all seemed to come up with the same result: I was fighting a battle with what I was beginning to learn was gender dysphoria or a general sense that I was, at my core, female.

I don't know what led me to it, but at one point, I decided that while my wife and kids were away, I would venture into the closet (I know, ironic, isn't it?) and try on a dress of my wife's just to see what it felt like. I really can't describe the sense of euphoria that came from that, but there it was - and I knew. I looked at myself in the mirror, her dress hanging off of the skeleton of a frame that was my body ravaged by AIDS, and I knew. The tears welled up again in my eyes as I finally spoke the words to myself: *this* is who I am.

CHAPTER TWELVE

The weeks began to go by, and with each day my strength began to return. I hadn't told my wife about what I had been discovering; rather, I simply began reading whatever I could find during the time she went to work and the kids were at school. With each passing day, though, this new revelation became increasingly clear.

The excitement and joy that I felt when wearing my wife's dress made me begin to wonder what it would be like to wear something that was closer to my size. I took one of my first trips out of the house on my own to look for something to wear that fit me. I went to the discount clothing store around the corner from my house. I didn't know what I'd find, but I had to feel that feeling once again.

The chime rang as I walked through the front door, and as I looked around, the nerves began to set in. What in the world was I doing here? Were they going to say anything about a guy who was looking at women's clothing? My palms began to sweat, and paused for a moment, wondering if this was all a mistake.

I took a deep breath and walked towards the activewear section. As I browsed through the clothes, it hit me - I had no clue how to shop for women's clothes. The only thing I did know, from shopping with my wife, that women's sizes were completely different in this mysterious realm of female apparel. I glanced down at the pair of leggings I had stopped at and quickly glanced around to see if anyone was paying attention to me. The price tag read $5.99, and the price made gave me confidence. I could do this.

I grabbed a grey knit dress to go with the leggings. I knew better than to think about trying them on, so I quickly glanced at the store's return policy while standing in line to check out at the front register. My palms began sweating, as I glanced around nervously to see if I was catching the attention of anyone, holding these clothing items in my trembling hands. Would they wonder if it was for me? I could tell them that it was for my wife. After all, I was wearing my wedding ring.

"Next customer!" called the cashier, startling me from my apprehensive reverie.

Stepping forward, I placed the items on the counter as she removed the inventory tags and scanned them. Somehow, I paid for the items without embarrassing myself, hopped in the car, and rushed home to try my new clothes on.

While the dress was a little on the small side, the leggings were perfect. I drew in my breath.

The rest of my morning sped by. I made myself lunch, watched a little more TV, and took another nap. I glanced down at my watch. Almost time to pick the kids up from school. I took the leggings off, tucked everything into the back of a drawer, changed into a pair of jeans, and headed out the door. I had actually survived my first time buying women's clothing.

It was like I had found a new drug: shopping for new things to wear. Strange, I hated shopping for clothes before. And while I had limited my own budget to the discount store around the corner and the local thrift store, the thrill was still there, and I decided to try and understand what this all meant by seeing if I could be comfortable following where this was leading me. But where was that? And was I wise to follow what felt like a deep intuition, or merely acting foolishly in the grip of compulsion, as I had so many years before?

Two weeks passed. I was happy exploring and experimenting with my new identity, but I also knew that this wasn't something I could keep secret. After all, I had seen where secrets led, and I definitely didn't want to do that to my wife again. But how to do this? Once again, I looked to the almighty all-knowing Google to find some sort of help to navigate what my next steps should be.

I looked up "what to do when you think you're transgender." "I think I'm transgender. Where should I go?" "Is there support for being transgender?" And suddenly, the listing for the Fresno LGBT Center was staring me back in the face. Now, I know what you might be thinking: Fresno has LGBTQ+ people? Let alone a center? Well, let's not get into that shall we, other than to say that if you want to help reopen a center in Fresno, the need is there.

I threw on a pair of shorts and a t-shirt and made the short drive to the small office that housed the local LGBT Center. I don't even remember how many times I circled the block debating on whether or not I should actually go through with it. My hands began shaking, and I remember looking back and forth, wondering if I would see somebody who might recognize me walking in.

"This is silly," I thought. "It's not like I'm going to buy drugs. Nobody's going to see. Just park, Darryl. You owe it to yourself."

And with that, a parking space opened up just around the corner from the front door. I parked, took a deep breath, and made the walk into the center. Even though it was only a few blocks, it felt like a mile. My nerves were heightened. My heart was beating out of my chest. I rushed up the steps and into the door, looking behind me to make sure that nobody saw me go in.

"Can I help you?," asked a deep yet feminine voice from behind the counter. Behind the desk sat a gorgeous young woman, either of a Mediterannean or South American descent.... Her caramel skin was smooth and her dark wavy hair hung down around her shoulders.

"Um....," I paused. I didn't think I could go through with this. I didn't want the first person I told to be this beautiful stranger. "I'm just looking, thank you."

"Okay. Let me know if you need anything."

I glanced at the pamphlets and flyers on the shelf. I picked up a copy of the community progressive newspaper and glanced through it.

"Is this your first time here?"

I nodded.

"What brings you in?"

"Well... I... I... I think I might be...." my voice trailed off. I couldn't even get the words out. "I'm struggling with thinking I'm... I think I might be transgender." There. It was finally out there. I exhaled.

"Oh, honey!," exclaimed the woman, rushing out from behind the counter. She threw her arms around me and congratulated me. "I'm Ramona," she said, extending her hand.

"Darryl," I replied, taking her hand.

Ramona showed me the different brochures they had, telling me about the support groups that they offered. She took me to the center's clothing closet, where people had donated articles of clothing for the taking. I spent the next hour browsing through the clothes, books, and flyers that they had at the center. The nerves had subsided, but in its place was a nervousness. I had opened Pandora's box.

CHAPTER THIRTEEN

"God, please... I don't want this to be me."

That was the prayer that would be almost like a daily mantra to me for the next week. And while other things began bringing hope around me - including a couple of former clients that decided to hire me as a freelance artist for them - much of my life was clouded by the combination of my recovery from the AIDS virus and the discovery that was starting to become clearer and clearer in my head. And the more and more I fought it, the more and more the picture became clearer - this thing I had been struggling against all my life? It was my true identity. There was a woman inside of me that was struggling to get free - and the glimpse that I gave her at freedom back at the LGBTQ+ center was something I couldn't undo.

But how would I manage this change? I mean, even being away from the church for so long, I still held onto a faith in God and in Jesus. And after this near-death experience, how I wanted to be sure of God's forgiveness. From what I knew of my faith in the conservative Evangelical community, coming out as LGBTQ+ was highly frowned upon. It was like a death knell, sealing me away from God forever - the unpardonable sin.

"But Darryl," I would argue with myself, "you've been away from church for this long, and you don't really miss it, do you? I mean, yeah, you're playing piano for a church at the moment, but they're not really the type of church you're talking about, is it? Can't you just find a home and faith that would work with them?"

"I know, but I feel like I just need some sort of affirmation from God that this is okay. I'm not in a good place right now, and I can't lose that."

"What will it take? Some sort of sign?"

"Perhaps."

It's funny how God hears that as a sort of prayer at times. That next weekend, as I played the piano for the local United Methodist Church, the pastor gave a sermon that centered around accepting and supporting the LGBTQ+ community. There it was. It was almost as if God had heard my request and this was his way of saying, "I give you permission. I see you. And I love you just as I created you - it's time to love the you I created, as well." I sighed. I knew what I had to do.

That night, my wife and I were snuggled on the couch in our pajamas playing our normal nighttime ritual of "what to watch on TV tonight?" I stretched my legs out down the length of the couch, my head resting on her chest as she wrapped her arms around me. I knew that I had to tell her, but what would it do to our marriage? My thoughts flickered back through the 17 years we had spent together - the awkward moment on her front balcony early on in our dating life as I was preparing to leave her apartment back to Southern California after a visit when I blurted out the question, "would you marry me?" The laughter that our oldest had together in the early years as a toddler. The first time I held our two younger children in my arms, their tiny eyes looking up into mine for the first time. The tears that flowed as we held each other following our two miscarriages. The sense of pride we had at purchasing our first home. There were so many memories and feelings flooding through me, and in an instant, I knew that the words I was about to speak would change everything and overshadow all over those memories. It was then that the tears started coming.

"What's the matter, honey?," she asked, gently stroking my head as the sniffles turned into full-on sobs.

"Well...," I choked out, trying to catch my breath and regain my composure. The reality of what I was about to do began to kick in, but then again, this was the woman who had, just months earlier, walked with me through the revelation that I was HIV positive — and not only that but that I had contracted it while cheating on her at a gay bathhouse. "Remember how we were having that conversation about who I am?"

"Yeah...?" She shifted, and I sat up, allowing me to look her in the eyes. Oh, those beautiful blue eyes that captured my heart almost two decades earlier.

"Well, I've been doing some research. And I think I'm coming to terms with the possibility that I'm transgender."

There it was. Out there. The silence felt like forever.

"You're what?"

"Transgender. I think I was meant to really be a woman."

Silence. The arms that had been embracing me and stroking my head fell limp.

"Liz?"

"I think I'm going to need some space."

We both began to cry. This isn't how I wanted our marriage to end, but at this point I was powerless. I got up from the couch and walked away, wondering if this would be the last time I would feel those arms around me. The arms that kept me safe for the past 17 years through the pain, sadness, and joy.

The self-criticism began to pour in:

"What have I done?"

"What were you even expecting, Darryl? First you give her the news that you have AIDS, then you tell her that you cheated on her, and now this? She's not going to get over this one."

"Why couldn't I have just kept silent?"

"I've hidden this for 40 years so far. Why not the rest of my life? I have a family, a home, a life…"

I paused at the threshold to the room.

"Liz?"

"Yes?"

"If you say that you're not okay with me being transgender, just say the word. I'll forget all of this," I said, trying hard to hold back the tears. "Just tell me."

She buried her head in the pillow that had taken my place in her lap.

"Please, just tell me."

"I just need some time."

Time. At least it wasn't a request to leave the house. In many ways, that probably would have been easier. But for the time being, it's all I had, and I had to find the hope in that. I crawled into bed and snuggled against my body pillow, praying that someone out there would hear me.

"God? Are you up there? Are you even listening?" I prayed. "If you can hear me, just, please... please save my marriage. Forgive me for being so incredibly stupid with my life." I began to cry again. "I've completely made a mess of everything you've entrusted to me. Show me what to do."

I tried to muffle the cries with my pillow until exhaustion took over. It was a few more hours until I felt the bed move as Liz climbed into the bed beside me. I held my breath, wondering if she would embrace me and hold me like she normally would as we went to sleep, but nothing. My mind started thinking about worst-case scenarios when the thought entered into my mind: "perhaps it would be best if I just succumbed to the AIDS virus." That'd be easy. There'd be less shame in that. After all, I had been on death's doorstep a couple of months ago, and it was just like going to sleep.

The bed began to shift again, and suddenly I felt my wife's hand touch my waist. I backed my body up against hers, and her arm pulled me in. I was safe, at least for another night. She had saved me.

CHAPTER FOURTEEN

I woke up as the sunlight began its attempt to peek through the small window in the door to the back yard. At some point in the middle of the night, we both rolled over to our own sides of the bed and against our own body pillows. I rolled back towards her in the bed, propping myself up, and kissed her gently on the cheek.

"Mmmmm," she responded.

"Good morning, my love."

"Thanks, hon. Are the kids up?"

"I don't know. I just woke up myself."

"Isn't it time to get them to school soon?"

"About. I'll get up now." I shifted to get out of bed and paused for a moment. "I love you."

"I know."

I know. Those words cut through the moment, making me wonder if things were really okay. If I had finally crossed the final bridge to signify the end of my marriage. The end of everything as I knew it.

I was brought up to believe that marriage was forever, no matter what. That the commitment I would make in marriage meant that I was bound "till death do us part." I couldn't let my marriage end this way. We had made it through the worst fears of the AIDS virus as the medication had helped my body make an almost miraculous recovery over the past three months. We were working through the issues of my infidelity and what that meant. I couldn't let this be the end. In my desperation, I reminded her: "You know, Liz, if you don't want me to act at all on this, let me know. I can't lose you."

Silence.

I threw some clothes on, walked out of the room, made sure the children were up and getting ready for school, made myself a cup of coffee in the Keurig, and sat at my desk to glance at what type of junk mail and social media posts were waiting to greet me. The routine of the morning seemed typical, but it still felt like everything had changed. How could that be?

I opened a browser tab on the computer, navigated the mouse to the search bar, and began to type: "trans women married." Stories began to fill my screen of couples who had navigated the coming out and transition of one spouse from male to female. At first glance, it seemed like, while difficult, there was a 50/50 chance of my marriage surviving. I began to hope that since my marriage had seemingly survived the battle with AIDS and pain of infidelity that our marriage was in the half that would survive.

"But how do you think Liz would do with being seen as a lesbian? Do you think she's ready for that? What about the kids?" The thoughts sprung into my head. I didn't know, and the unknown without any means of control was beginning to be the scariest part of this whole journey. I began to wish that there was some way to take it all back; to go back to the way it was and forget this had ever become a thought in my head.

"Dad! Are you ready to go?"

The voice of my middle child rescued me from the downward spiral that my thoughts had become.

"Yeah - let me just grab my keys," I said, grabbing my keys and wallet off of the desk. "Hey - sweet child of mine! Make sure you're ready to go when I get back!"

"Okay!" came the call from the other room.

We headed out the door. The trip to drop off the kids at their respective high schools was uneventful, and I returned to my wife who was getting ready for her day, and our oldest son, who was still in bed as young adults do.

I returned to the kitchen, brewed a second cup of coffee, said goodbye to Liz as she headed out the door, and sat back down at my desk. An e-mail from a former client at the agency I used to work for caught my attention:

"Darryl — we worked with you before and were really happy with your work. As we're not really happy with the designer that took your spot, we're interested in hiring you to continue developing our graphics and email blasts. Would you be interested?"

The thought had never crossed my mind. For a good portion of the day, I considered the idea of starting my own agency for web and graphic design. What would that look like? I took out post-it notes and began writing ideas on what my business would entail, stopping only for lunch and to pick the kids up from school. By the time my wife came home from work, I was ready to greet her with the news.

"Liz — guess what?"

"Um… what?" I took a step back, as her face shifted from weariness after a long day at work to concern. "Is there more that you need to tell me?"

"Oh — yes — but nothing like that."

"Then what?"

"I got an email from a past client asking me if I'd do some work for them because they liked my work."

"Oh! Do you think you're going to do that?"

"Yes, and I think on top of that, I might start my own business doing this — I sat in on enough pitch meetings and have done these projects from start to finish. There's no sense in needing to work for a company when I could be doing it on my own."

"Well, what would you call it?"

"I'm not sure yet."

"Well, anything you can do to help bring money in would be good."

"Great."

"Do you have dinner started?"

"Um…"

"Darryl!"

"I'll get it started now."

I put everything down and threw the ground turkey into skillet and noodles into a pot for the evening's dinner of spaghetti with meat sauce. What was I going to name this business? More than that, what was the name I was going to take on if I transitioned? There was so much to think about, but at the moment, the browning meat on the stove was going to take priority.

With dinner finished and the kids working on their homework, Liz and I took up our normal spots on the couch.

"So," she began, "have you thought at all about what your name is going to be?"

"Not really," I replied. "Gertrude," I said jokingly.

She playfully pushed me back. "Get out of here. Seriously."

"I honestly don't know. I like Kim."

Her nose wrinkled.

"I don't know. I'm still thinking." Then it hit me. "Does this mean that you're okay with this?"

"Well, not okay," she said, "but I'm open to talking about it."

"Then, if you don't mind, I found a documentary on HBO that I'd like to watch. I was waiting in hopes that we could watch it together."

"Um.... sure."

We spent the next hour watching The Trans List on HBO, a collection of transgender people who share their stories and experiences of struggle and coming out to embrace their truth. By the time it was finished, I don't think I had any tears left. I had started sobbing from the first story and didn't stop until well after it was over.

I turned to my wife, and through my tears said, "I really don't know how or what. I don't know how this would even happen. All I know is that I don't want to hide this from you. And I want to work through this with you. I love you, Liz, and this doesn't change that. It doesn't mean that I'm going to fully embrace living as a woman, but I at least needed to get this out there so we can talk about it."

Again, silence. "How long have you… I mean, have you done anything to…?" her quivering voice trailed off. I saw the fear forming in her eyes.

I began a series of confessions to her, where I would walk her through the stories of my youth. The questions that surrounded me. The way that I tried to hide it in religion. How I began struggling with it over the last week. How it felt to try on her dress. And how it felt to wear the leggings that I had bought and hidden away.

"You bought leggings?"

"Yeah."

"Go put them on."

"I don't know, I…"

"No, go put them on."

I got up from the couch, went to the bedroom, and emerged, sheepishly, in the grey pair of leggings that I had purchased. She patted the seat next to her on the couch, motioning for me to sit.

"Wait. Stand right there."

She pulled out her phone, and I stood there, horrified, as she took a photo.

"Okay, now sit."

I sat and watched as she posted something to Facebook.

"What are you -" I grabbed towards her phone. She wasn't going to out me to the world, was she?

"Shh." She pulled back out of my reach, and turned the phone around to show me. Her Facebook post simply read this: "My wife is really hot in leggings."

I smiled, my heart full, and snuggled in next to her. Everything was going to be okay.

CHAPTER FIFTEEN

Over the next several weeks, this new revelation became the center of our conversation. To my own surprise, with more research, Liz not only accepted me but embraced my newfound quest for womanhood. But what would that look like?

Liz had gone to work and, as per the usual, Chris was still asleep in his bed, and as I sat at my desk, a pile of paperwork fell off and onto the floor. Not surprising, as my desk had become the catch-all for everything in the house.

"Dad, where do you want these papers from school?"

"Put it on my desk."

"The mail?"

"Desk."

"The newspaper?"

You get the picture. This morning, it seems as though I was going to have to take on the sporadic task of sorting through the papers to decide their different fates: trash, file, or shredder. The shuffling of papers attracted our giant Siberian Tabby cat, Shroedinger, who decided that it was an invitation to play. A few belly rubs and a snuggle later, he was off to wander the house while I looked at the different piles I had created. I stood up, brushed the fur off of me, and then opened the file drawers to start putting away insurance papers and such. As I did, a single folder caught my attention at the back of the drawer: writing portfolio. It was a folder I had created in high school to keep some of my writing assignments over the years. I pulled it out, unsure of what I would find.

The folder itself was a trip down memory lane, and as I held the red cardstock in my hands, I thought of Mrs. Zieg, who told us to hold onto this, keeping our writing from the year and anything we wanted to hold onto as a writing sample, in case we needed it after college. If she only knew. I opened the folder, and a few papers in I found a couple pages of binder paper, faded and yellowed, paper clipped together, filled with handwritten words in pencil. I looked closer and began to read: it was one of my stories about Ellie from my sophomore year in high school.

It was a welcome distraction. I sat in the middle of the mess on the carpet and began to read, giggling at the references to Pearl Jam and music writing. Three pages into the manuscript, and it suddenly hit me: I am Ellie. The words that poured off of my pencil and onto these pages those years ago were my attempt to see the world and live my life through Ellie's eyes, down to her desire to attend the California Institute of the Arts, the school where I spent my first semester of college as a music major — just like Ellie. It was fate.

"Ellie," I sighed. I knew the name I would choose, and just like Ellie, the formal name would be Eleanor Anne — a name she despised but held onto as needed for formality. "Ellie," I repeated. Everything had begun to make sense.

I quickly gathered up the rest of the papers, shredded the shred pile, and finished filing the others away. I sat at my desk and began to try and figure out what life would be like with my new identity. I sat and began doodling the name on a piece of scrap paper.

Later that evening, Liz and I were settling into bed for the night, my back snuggled into her body and her arms wrapped tenderly around me.

"Liz?"

"Yes, hon?"

"I love you."

"I love you too."

I twisted around and out of her embrace to kiss her gently.

"I've been thinking about names."

"And?" she asked skeptically.

"Well, the name I've chosen is Eleanor Anne."

Her nose crinkled in disgust and her eyes searched mine to see if I was really serious or not.

I smiled. "But I want to go by Ellie."

The immediate sense of judgment in her face began to fade away as she started mulling it over in her head.

I recounted the events of the morning, and how it just seemed to make sense.

"Ellie," she sighed as we settled back into our gentle embrace.

I smiled. It felt wonderful to hear my wife speak my name for the first time.

"But really... Eleanor?" she asked.

"Yes."

"Okay, Ellie." There it was again.

"I love you, Liz."

"Have you given any thought as to how we're going to tell everyone in our lives?"

"Not yet."

"Well, we have Chris' graduation coming up. If you're going to start presenting as female, we're going to need to figure out how to start making this public."

"Yeah."

It was one thing to have to come out to Liz, but one of the things I hadn't thought about since I had been spending so much time at home recovering from my battle with AIDS was the fact that this was going to be a very public-facing change to my life. How was that going to work?

"Do you have any ideas?" I asked.

Liz pushed me gently aside and sat up in the bed, grabbing her iPhone and opening it to the notes app.

"Let's think about who we need to tell first," she started.

"I don't know... our parents... my sister..."

Within a few minutes, we had a full but still incomplete list of people. We had the who, now we had to figure out the when. With some of the upcoming events on the calendar, we knew that it was going to have to be a couple of months until I could start openly embracing my new life as Ellie.

The biggest of these was an annual musical production that I had been working with for several years. While many theatre groups are supportive of the LGBTQ+ community, the entire cast was over the age of 55, and involved in the more conservative areas of Fresno. We had been working on the production for over a year; I couldn't risk throwing everything off by fully coming out before the end of our production in June.

At the same time, certain changes probably could be made in preparation of my public change. First up on the list was clothing. While dresses were still a ways away for me, it was decided that I could try shopping for jeans and t-shirts in the women's section. Now, that might not seem like much, but for a 40-year-old man who had never shopped in the women's section before, it was terrifying. Yes, I had shopped in the women's section at the discount store, but people we knew shopped at Target, which is where my wife insisted we go.

I followed my wife through the front doors and, after grabbing a cart, made the quick left towards the women's clothing department, the entire time glancing all around me to make sure I didn't see anyone I recognized. I think she sensed my nervousness because she grabbed the cart and started looking at t-shirts, jeans, and jean shorts. That had to be harmless, right? I mean, guys wear them too, right? We settled on a few shirts, a pair of jeans, and a couple of pairs of shorts, after which my wife started guiding me towards — of all places — the dressing rooms. Now, at our Target, the dressing rooms were gender-neutral, so I remained calm until I realized I had to show the clothes to the attendant.

THAT freaked me out.

"Okay, you need to try these on before we buy them."

"But, I..." my hands were shaking and my voice was quivering.

"Go!," she said, putting the clothes into my arms and pushing me towards the woman behind the counter.

I took a deep breath and started walking towards the counter, continuously alternating glances between the shoppers behind me who were oblivious to the major life change that was about to happen a few feet away and my wife, who was waiting impatiently, motioning me with her eyes for me to go in.

"Can I help you?" asked the attendant.

"Um.... yes.... I'd like to..." My voice trailed off.

"I'm sorry?"

"I'd like to try these on," I said, trying to avoid eye contact.

She took the clothes from my hands, counted them, and handed them back with a number tag.

"Okay, here you go."

It only took me about ten minutes to try on all of the clothes, after which I chose the pair of jeans, one pair of shorts and a couple of shirts, returned the rest and the tag to the counter, and hurried out of the dressing rooms.

"That wasn't that bad, was it?," asked my wife, who seemed amused by my embarrassment.

"Shut up." I threw the clothes into the cart and started walking off.

"Wait," she said, starting to head in the other direction.

"Where are you...?" My mistake. I thought we were going to take this one step at a time, and I had been hoping that the dressing room was going to be the big step of the night. I was wrong. I watched in horror as my wife started taking the cart and walking towards the bra section. Thankfully I got away with not having to try that on, so there's that.

That night, I walked out of the store with a strange sense of comfort. No, the terror I felt was real, but I lived through this experience and even found some new feminine clothes. And if I could live through this experience, then perhaps it was more in my own head than I realized. Perhaps the fears of being publicly outed and embarrassed were unfounded. Either way, it was done. I survived another step in my own transformation, and that was cause for hope.

Writing this three years later, I wish I could say those nerves have entirely subsided. They haven't. I still feel panicked from time to time. While I feel more comfortable about myself and my body, I wonder if the question of what others are thinking about me will ever go away. Time will tell.

CHAPTER SIXTEEN

"Excuse me, but I think you're in the wrong restroom."

My body went cold and my muscles tightened. This is the moment I had been dreading since beginning my public transformation to Ellie. I attempted a smile, nodded, and hurried out of the restroom.

"The women's restroom is over there" the man called after me as I rushed into the lobby as if my reddening cheeks weren't enough to embarrass me.

Four months had passed since the experience in Target. Our senior production had completed its run. My oldest child graduated from high school. I had come out publicly in almost every area of my life and had begun living openly as Ellie. I had graduated from the tedious task of learning to paint my own nails and have moved onto getting acrylics at the local nail salon. I began to grow my hair out from the short crew cut I had sported for most of my married life and it was starting to take on a life of its own. Most importantly, I had started on a daily regimen of estrogen supplements and testosterone blockers, and the name on my driver license and IDs now read Eleanor. This was really happening, and the changes were happening daily.

As part of a season ticket package to the theatre in Los Angeles, we had made the three-hour trek from Fresno to see The Curious Incident of the Dog in the Nighttime. We met up with my mother, who shortly after coming out to her told me, "just promise me that you won't use the women's bathroom." So, in an effort to avoid that conversation, I proceeded to use the men's bathroom this time, despite the fact that I was dressed in a flowing pink blouse with a stuffed bra accented by my crossbody brown satchel, a pair of black Pixie pants from Old Navy, and a pair of black wedges. My hair was blow-dried and styled, makeup was applied, and a pair of dangling rose-gold earrings completed the ensemble. No, this wasn't the look that one would expect to find in the men's bathroom.

So when I heard the words, "excuse me, but I think you're in the wrong restroom," I knew exactly what he meant. He and I both knew, though I honestly think that he believed it to be more of an innocent mistake made by a woman rather than a transgender woman who wasn't quite sure of herself to use the women's restroom in a public setting.

Up until this point, my trips out of the house had to be meticulously planned based on the proximity to local Starbucks stores, as I knew that the restrooms at their locations were single-stall and non-gender specific. This incident just reinforced in my mind why I would put in such a concerted effort into this practice. After all, if my own mother would be offended at my using the women's restroom, what would happen in the minds of women who didn't know me?

"You're crazy, Ellie," I thought. "This is the theatre in Los Angeles. People from all walks of life are here. If anyone is going to be accepting of the trans community, it's going to be the people here. If you need to use the women's restroom, you should be able to." Yet the fear remained, and I made it a point to avoid going to the restroom again until we had left the theatre and found a gender-neutral single-stall restroom to use before dinner.

The first time I would actually use the women's restroom wouldn't come until a while later when shopping at Target. Someone was using the gender-neutral family restroom… and I needed to go.

"Just go in the women's bathroom!" said Liz.

"I don't know if I'm ready to do that."

"Sooner or later, you're going to need to get over that fear."

I knew she was right, but the fears that consumed my head — fears that weren't unfounded, as I had been telling myself. Stories flood the news of trans women who looked a LOT more womanly than I that were publicly shamed and humiliated because another person took it upon themselves to point out that they were trans. Threats on message boards talk about husbands who would want to kill or maim trans women who would dare to use the same restrooms as their wives and daughters. And it wasn't just limited to other parts of the nation. The restroom debate was something that had become a regular item of discussion on local talk radio. For me, using the restroom was an ordeal. I couldn't use the men's room as I was, but the fear that came from using the women's restroom was paralyzing.

"Would you like for me to go with you?"

I nodded, wide-eyed, and shaking.

"Well, come on!" she motioned, stepping toward the door. When I didn't move, she grabbed my arm and pulled me in.

I rushed in, eyes towards the floor, found a stall, and quickly closed the door. I sat quietly, listening for just the slightest sound of a breath that would signify that another person was in here with me, my mind racing as I tried to imagine every worst-case scenario that I might find.

"What if someone accuses me?" I thought to myself. All it would take is one accusation. No trial; no proof. Just an accusation that I was trying to be inappropriate in the women's bathroom and my life would be over.

I had seen the stories — trans people who had been publicly shamed and embarrassed as they're escorted from stores across the US just because someone had accused them of being in the wrong bathroom. Trans women who were just like me who found themselves the focus of a viral video in today's social-media-driven world. Husbands who have threatened, beaten and even killed trans women who dared to use the same bathroom as their wives and daughters.

I braced myself for the coming onslaught of what I was sure to find, but nothing came. I pulled some toilet paper out and threw it in the toilet as I struggled to hide my penis in case a curious person were to glance through the gap between the door and partition of the restroom. I flushed the toilet, took a deep breath, and rushed out of the stall towards the sinks. I didn't even wait for Liz. I simply washed my hands and moved as quickly out and away from the door, as if I was culpable for even standing near the women's restroom. I sighed, my heart racing, praying that nobody was going to call me out on what I had just done, and wondering if I had even taken a breath while I was inside.

"Please, God, let this get easier," I prayed. Surely, it had to. I couldn't live the rest of my life around Starbucks visits.

CHAPTER SEVENTEEN

Weeks and months went by, and with it came new experiences and new discoveries, not to mention a list of things that needed to happen on my journey towards fully being Ellie. I had begun growing my hair out, and had begun getting more and more feminine in my clothing choices — including a padded bra — and conversations were underway to add my name to waiting lists for surgery.

Calls were increasing for my freelance work and the HIV virus went from overwhelming to undetectable thanks to medication and modern science. I also began taking steps to establish my freelance web and graphic design work as an actual business with a name which embraced my new status in the world: EllieGirl. My business would be based on the idea that I would be helping people celebrate their identity through design that truly represented and told their story. And yet, as I began to take these steps, I had no clue what I was doing. It was seriously a step of faith, but I was certain that this was what God was calling me towards - and yes, I get how that sounds with the fact that I wasn't in church at the time.

Looking back, I can definitely see God's fingerprints all over it, but I wouldn't know that until almost a year later. I began listening to podcasts on what it would take to run a business, and, trying to narrow the field down, discovered the world of female entrepreneurship. It was like my earlier days in the Evangelical church. However, rather than soaking up Bible teachings, I began learning about establishing a business, writing a business plan, and most importantly, networking. I decided that - if I was serious about doing this as a business - I would have to begin networking.

One morning, after the children had been taken to school and Liz had gone off to her job, I sat at my desk with a fresh cup of coffee and turned Spotify on. The acoustic sounds of Diana Krall and the aroma of caffeinated French Vanilla coffee began to fill the room as I settled into the black pleather of my swivel desk chair. The warm glow of the dual 28" monitors on my desk illuminated with a couple of clicks of the mouse as I logged in to the computer and began my morning routine of checking emails and social media.

I scrolled through my Facebook feed, skimming the various updates and funny memes that my friends had posted throughout the evening and morning, giggling to myself while sipping the coffee out of my custom printed pink EllieGirl branded mug. This morning, as I scrolled, a sponsored ad caught my attention for a coworking group for women that was meeting the following Thursday at a coffee house in town. I quickly clicked on the interested button, which led me to a page that explained the event as a gathering of entrepreneurial women from around the Fresno area that were looking for a way to connect with others. A few more clicks connected me with Kayla, the group's leader via chat.

"I RSVP'd for the coffeehouse meeting, but will my presence there be a problem as a trans woman?"

"I don't believe it will be."

"Well, great! I can't wait to meet you!"

"I can't wait to meet you!"

And so it was set that Ellie was about to hit the public stage as I planned to take my business and venture out for the first time. While I had gained support from most of my online friends, I couldn't help but wonder what the public response was going to be.

"Well, I'm not going to worry about that now," I thought as I went to add the event to my online calendar. As I began to type the address into the location bar, my heart dropped. The gathering was happening in a coffeehouse on the campus of an Evangelical church. What was I walking into?

Trying to think of a way to backpedal out of the meeting, I opened up the chat box again and messaged Kayla again.

"Kayla — I just noticed that your meeting is going to be happening at the Frappe House. That's at a church, right?"

"Yes."

"Are you sure it's not going to be a problem that I'm there?"

"It shouldn't be."

"I'm really not sure if I should."

"Well, I don't want you to be uncomfortable, but I can't imagine that it'd be a problem. We're not affiliated with the church at all, and all of our ladies are wonderful. It's just one of the larger spots in the area with free wifi and good coffee."

"Okay, as long as you think it's going to be safe."

"Don't worry, I'll watch for you."

"Okay. See you next Thursday, then."

"Sounds good!"

Before I knew it, the day had arrived. I packed up my laptop in my newly embroidered EllieGirl bag, went to the bathroom (because God knows I didn't want to have to go there), shaved off the facial hair shadow, and did my makeup. I glanced at myself in the mirror. The hormones had begun their work, and even behind the padded sports bra, small breasts buds had begun to form on my chest. My features were softening, and my hair was noticeably longer. I threw on a white t-shirt with EllieGirl printed on the front, a pair of jeans, and finished the ensemble off with a pair of pink earrings and heeled boots.

I checked my lipstick in the mirror before tucking it away in my dusty pink crossbody purse, grabbed the keys out, and headed out the door to my white GMC Safari. It was a bit of a drive across town to the coffeehouse, which was located in the middle of what is known as "church row" in North Fresno, so I turned on a mix of music on my phone in an attempt to distract my mind from all of the "what if" scenarios that were trying to take over my thoughts.

"You say… you only hear what you want to…" I was singing along to one of my all-time favorite songs as I pulled into the parking lot: Stay (You Missed Me) by Lisa Loeb and the Nine Stories.

The song finished as I found a parking spot, and then as I turned the car off and the music stopped, the anxiety hit as though the music was a dam that was holding back a flood of fears that suddenly came rushing in a torrent of worry once it was gone. I worked hard to focus on Kayla's words to me: "Don't worry. I'll watch for you."

Opening Facebook, I saw that the update form the event said that the women were starting to arrive. I took a deep breath, grabbed my bag from the passenger seat, my purse, and slid out of the van.

"Take a step, Ellie," I thought to myself as my body froze. I looked up, and it felt like the coffeehouse was a million miles away. I locked the car, and began to walk in, praying to God that I'd survive the morning without becoming the subject of a viral video.

I stepped through the doorway and looked around the expansive room, allowing the delicious aroma of brewing coffee to fill my nostrils. Kayla wasn't wrong — the space was massive with large and small meeting tables in two levels, couches, and a small bookstore in the corner. One of the walls was composed by a clear roll-up garage-style door, which opened up to a courtyard with additional seating and the church's outdoor baptismal. Around the room, small groups and couples were gathered, many of them with Bibles opened while they sipped on their coffee and talked excitedly, their voices combining with the worship music playing through the loudspeakers in the room. A small gas fireplace on the wall by the counter was lit in front of two couches, and in the center of the room were two long tables with women who were working on laptops.

"That must be them," I thought as I started towards that side of the room. A young attractive woman with long blond hair looked up from her laptop and locked eyes with me. She smiled, waved, and got up from the table to start towards me, confirming my suspicions.

"You must be Ellie," she said, opening her arms for a hug.

"I am," I replied, hugging her back. "I'm glad I'm in the right place,"

I joked.

She laughed. "Yes, you are. The group is over here," she said, motioning to the long tables where three other women were working. The women were varied in age, one with short gray hair dressed in business casual wear, another woman who looked to be closer to my age with shoulder-length dirty blonde hair was in a t-shirt and jeans. There was another woman who was closer to Kayla's age with long dark hair was hunched over her Macbook Pro with her back to us as we approached the table.

"Michelle!" called Kayla, and immediately the woman looked up from her Macbook and looked over at us. "I want you to meet Ellie. She's going to be joining us today."

She. It was the one of the first times I had heard myself referred to as female, and the recognition of that stunned me.

"Hi, Ellie," said Michelle, extending her hand. "I'm Michelle, and these are the women of Her Space," she said, motioning to the two other women at the table. "There's Gina and Sheryl," she continued, introducing the women.

"Nice to meet you."

"Ellie runs a graphic design and website design business," Kayla informed the group. I nodded. "And Michelle," she said, turning back to me, "is helping me run our little coworking group."

"It's really great to be here today," I said, smiling at the women, and setting my bags down at the table. "If you'll excuse me, I'm going to go grab a cup of coffee."

As the morning went on, a few more women joined us, and others left, and as I started meeting other women who simply welcomed me into their community, the fears began to dissipate. Before long, I found myself joking and socializing with the women as we worked on the various projects that we had brought with us. Around lunchtime, the group began leaving one by one, until it was Kayla, Michelle, and I.

"Well, I think we're going to grab lunch," said Kayla, looking at Michelle and closing the lid to her laptop. "Ellie, would you like to join us?"

"Sure!"

After deciding on a local sushi restaurant, we gathered our belongings and left the coffeehouse for lunch.

The three of us spent another hour together sharing stories. Kayla told me how a similar coworking group had saved her own sanity as a telecommuter in San Diego a few years back, and how when she returned to the Fresno area, she was intent on creating a similar space for the women in the area with the future goal to secure an actual office space where coworking could happen 24/7 for women all over the Central Valley. In turn, I shared my own story, allowing them to ask me any questions they might have.

"What has your experience been like since beginning your transition?" asked Michelle.

"Well, to be honest, this is the first time I've really been out in public since coming out," I replied. "And it's been amazing — nothing like what I imagined it would be like."

Kayla laughed, telling Michelle about our first interactions online.

"You both have been wonderful to me," I continued, laughing along with them. "I honestly was expecting that I'd have to find a way to leave right away because I didn't know if I would actually be accepted as a woman."

"Well, I am glad that you're with us," said Kayla, Michelle nodding in agreement.

"As am I," I replied. "I feel like I've made some new friends today."

"You have," said Kayla, smiling at me. "I'll be your friend."

"As will I," said Michelle.

"Thank you, ladies," I replied, choking back tears of joy. "That means the world to me."

Kayla must have sensed the emotionality of the moment, as she got up from her seat and came over to give me a hug.

"Thank you," I repeated, hugging her back.

"Of course."

I had been seen. Me. Ellie. It felt amazing.

CHAPTER EIGHTEEN

Family. That one word alone conjures up so many ideas, so many pictures. For some, it's a wonderfully warm place. For others, it's a place of fear and comes with feelings of betrayal and pain. Still, others find themselves remembering a time when family meant something, and they've worked through the more recent years to redefine family not as those they are born into, but as those they have chosen. For the family of the Biblical parable of the prodigal son, the word family was complex.

My own experiences with family are complicated. I walked away from my home at the age of 22 to start a family of my own. I left the family that I had built in the Catholic church for a good chunk of my younger life to build a new family within the Evangelical church. When that family atmosphere became abusive, I lost everything. While I am attempting to find family again within the church, it's not always possible. In fact, many are telling me that it's never going to be possible as long as I am living as Ellie.

One year had passed since that first meeting with Kayla and the Her Space women, and since that time, I had become an active member of the Her Space family. I had launched my business and was spending a good chunk of my time at their new office space while my kids were in school.

One particular day, I was sitting across from a newer member, Rachel. She and I had connected earlier in the year over our appreciation for the book, Girl, Wash Your Face by Rachel Hollis, and we'd talk throughout the day about faith, encouraging each other to be better women and mothers. It was a fun friendship, and we often would sit and work at the same table in the office, Rachel in oversized sweaters and jeans, and I in my dresses.

"Ellie, what are you doing Friday night?," she asked from behind her laptop.

"Um, I don't know. Let me check my calendar.... Nope, it doesn't look like I have anything."

"Well, my church is holding a women's event, and I think you might enjoy it. I'd love for you to come."

I froze. Church. I thought back, trying to remember what my last experiences were in the church. Ten years. It had been ten years since I had even darkened the doorway of an Evangelical church. It was hard enough to start working at the local United Methodist Church as a paid musician. But attend an Evangelical Church service? For a women's event? Why — and how — would I even consider going?

"Um... I'm familiar with that church, Rachel," I started apologetically. "I don't think they'd let me through the doors, let alone welcome _"

"You're safe with me. I'm sure it'll be fine."

And just like that, I agreed to go to church with her that Friday night.

Getting out of the house that night was hard. The kids were arguing about something. Dinner was late being made. For a while, I contemplated not going and making an excuse. After all, Rachel would understand. Nevertheless, I carefully did my makeup and put on a flowy pink top and jeans along with a pair of heeled boots and looked at myself in the mirror. Feminine enough. Maybe they wouldn't notice. I grabbed my purse and my Bible and headed out the door.

My heart was beating out of my chest as I made the final turn into the church parking lot. I knew that God wanted me to be there that night, and Rachel was a good friend. But church? Really? Was this some sort of test? I sat in the parking lot for a little bit, watching the women stream into the church, and realized that I hadn't gone to the bathroom. Starbucks. There was a Starbucks across the street.

I started the car back up and quickly made the trek across the street to the Starbucks, all the while still trying not to seem suspicious as the nervousness had not worn off. I went to the bathroom, checked myself in the mirror, and proceeded back across the street to the church. I don't know how long I actually sat there in the parking lot, but it was a while. My fingers, still grasping the keys, kept moving between putting the keys into my purse and back into the ignition to drive away.

"Please, God - really?" I prayed silently, closing my eyes. "This is really you? You want me to do this?"

I opened my eyes to see Rachel pulling into the parking lot. She had spotted me, and was waving from her car. Too late. I couldn't turn back now. I threw my keys into the purse, and stepped out of the car, smiling nervously at my friend and waving back. To say I was a nervous wreck as I walked into the church building would be an understatement. I stuck by Rachel, afraid to make eye contact with anyone, and made my way with her to a seat.

Not much later, the worship band took the stage and sang:

"I'm no longer a slave to fear; I am a child of God. I'm no longer a slave to fear; I am a child of God."

It was the mantra I needed to hear. And from that point, the tears began to flow. I was home. God had welcomed me in with open arms.

CHAPTER NINETEEN

My more Charismatic Christian friends used to tell me about how "God spoke to them," as if there was an audible voice that they had access to. There's something unnerving about that when you're in a more traditional setting - because, after a while, you start wondering why you're not hearing from God. Like it's some sort of holiness test or something. I never believed in the flashing sign that He showed some believers to let you know which way to God. I believed God can help guide with gentle nudgings, but nothing like what I had heard from my Charismatic friends. That is, until now.

The tears were flowing down my face, and at first, I tried to wipe them away and hide it, but after a while, I just gave up. The first song ended, and the band took up the next chorus, inviting us to sing along:

I am chosen, not forsaken

I am who You say I am

You are for me, not against me

I am who You say I am

Who the Son sets free

Oh is free indeed

I am a child of God

Yes I am

In my Father's house

There's a place for me

I am a child of God

Yes I am

I am a child of God. I stood there, arms raised, tears streaming down my face, and I audibly heard God affirm that in me. It was as if the band was singing it directly to me, saying, "listen - no matter what anyone says, you are free, Ellie. You are my kid. And there's a place for you here."

"But how, Lord?," I replied back through my tears. "Look at me. I know what the church says about people like me. I remember what I used to say about people like me. There's no way I could have a place here."

"You know who you are in me. There's not going to be a way to control what others say about you, but remember this: You are loved. You are mine."

"Yes, Lord."

I didn't know how this was going to end up, but I do know that God met me there. The entire night was God. And here I was, met with the dilemma of knowing that God wanted me back in a church community, but not knowing how to do that as a queer trans woman. I walked out of the church that evening with Rachel, quietly arguing with God about how in the world this would even work. For the most part that evening, I was met with politeness. Only a few quizzical stares throughout the night served as a reminder to me that I didn't quite fit in. I looked away and shifted directions since I wasn't sure I wanted to find out how they would treat me if they had found out who I really was.

"Ellie - just ask!," I felt the nudging of God as I watched the women's ministry director walk out of the building and into the courtyard where I was standing.

"What do I say, though?"

"What is it that you want?"

"I'd love to have a community to belong to and grow."

"Well, ask."

I gathered the courage to approach her.

I took a step, and she started talking with someone. Whew. Saved for another moment.

I stood with Rachel and her friends for a while as I sipped on coffee, all the while watching to see where the director went. I took my eyes off of her for a few seconds to listen to one of the other women in our group and looked back to realize that I couldn't find her. I began to wonder if I had lost my opportunity, when I noticed that she had started walking in my direction.

"Um, Sandy?"

"Yes?"

"Hi," I blurted out, extending my free hand. "I'm Ellie, and I have to say that I really enjoyed tonight's meeting."

"Well, thank you, I'm glad," she smiled back. "I'm glad you were able to make it. Is this your first time here?"

"I was wondering if I could have a moment to talk with you in private."

"Sure!," she said, and she led me to a planter slightly away from the crowd.

Over the next half hour or so, I poured out my story, fighting back the tears. I shared how I had walked away from the church. How I had vowed never to return. And how God led me back that night. I talked about how I knew God wanted me back in community, and then asked the big question: "is this somewhere I could belong? Somewhere I could grow in my relationship with God and as a woman of God?"

As those words flowed out of my mouth, I felt the urging of God once more, as if I should take special note of those words. "Ellie, I want you to pay attention to this. Because THIS is what I am going to call you to do."

There was an awkward silence — so much so that I began to wonder if she had heard that voice too.

"Ellie," she began cautiously. "Thank you for sharing your story with me. I have to tell you that I appreciate your honesty and your bravery. I couldn't have been easy to share that with me. To be honest, I didn't think anything when I met you. I just thought you were one of the girls."

Had I really passed as a woman? Certainly, it wasn't something I saw when I looked in the mirror. I wondered if it was something I would ever see.

"I want you to know that God loves you. I know that He has a plan for you. It's not a mistake that you're here tonight — and I think you know that."

I nodded in response.

"The fact of the matter is, you're the first transgender person I've ever met. And while I don't doubt your sincerity, I don't know where to go from here. I'm going to talk with the pastors in my office tomorrow, and we'll have to get back to you. I'm sorry I can't give you an answer right now — but as I'm sure you know, this is a delicate situation, and I need to get counsel before I can give you an answer."

"Of course, Sandy," I said, the tears welling up in my eyes. "I honestly can't believe that you wouldn't run me out of here. That you aren't asking me to repent."

"Well, Ellie, you know what the Bible says. I can't deny that you have a faith in Jesus, and that you have His forgiveness. Your current way of living - that's between you and God. I'm just happy you were here tonight."

So am I, Sandy. So am I.

CHAPTER TWENTY

It was the next week when I got a call from the office at the church.

"Listen, I talked with the pastors here at the church, and I wanted to know if you'd be open to meeting with myself and one of our other pastors next week?"

I paused, wondering what this could possibly mean. I had heard stories of other LGBTQ+ people who had been confronted by church leaders and from there referred to reparative therapy. But here we were, and I had an audience with someone I could share my story with once again. Should I do this? Could I do it?

"Ellie, this is what I have called you to do." The words from God reverberated in my head.

"I know, God, but —"

"...But you know that I'm in control."

"Yes, Lord."

"Then I am with you. Don't be afraid. They need to see your faith and hear your story."

"Sandy — when would a good time be?"

I grabbed a pen and paper as we finalized the details of our meeting, and then added the appointment to the calendar. Things were starting to move, and while part of me was excited, part of me was terrified as to what I would find on the other side of the gaping divide that I saw between the LGBTQ+ community and the Church. From my training in college as well as in church before, I knew that there was going to be a huge emphasis on the Bible to try and refute anything that I would say. If I was going to stand a chance to gain an understanding, I was going to have to do so Biblically.

I already knew the overview of the theology that I embraced about who I was. That at the core of who I am, I was a bearer of the image of God. That God's original intention for me when I was being created was that I was to be a woman. That, because of sin and imperfections entering into the world, my physical body was a deformity — a mistake that happened in the DNA while I was being formed, and because of that, I was working now to bring my body more in line with what God had originally intended. If anything, that was what I was going to call them to consider.

After all, we use that explanation to help us grasp and answer the question of "does God create cancer?" Or, "why did God make my child autistic?" We often tell them, "well, I don't believe that God created them that way — I believe that He allowed it, but with the recognition that we live in a fallen world. A world with imperfection." So with that in mind, doesn't gender dysphoria fall into that category?

I sat back and thought about how I got here. The pastor I worked for who, rather than approaching me with questions about how I was running the ministries I was in charge of, took his concerns to public forums on the internet. How, when confronted with the information when I presented it to him — along with the answers to the questions he had been asking — the claim was made that his trust was betrayed. That I had no right to read what he had written under the assumption that the public forums would be hidden from my eyes.

The next pastor I would work for that would yell at and demean his staff on a regular basis. The times when I was called stupid or careless for missing things as small as an Oxford comma in the final proofs of the weekly bulletins that would be sent his way for approval. The countless hours and seven-day weeks I was asked to work in an effort to avoid making "Pastor" mad.

I thought about the pastors I had appreciated and learned from who had been disgraced by sexual sin. Pastors of mega-churches all over the country. Leaders I had respected. And in the midst of that, knowing that I was counted among them even before getting a chance to truly lead. How could God use me? How could I ever trust church again? Was I just setting myself up to be hurt again?

Then I thought about that one amazing night that had started all of this. Despite the nerves, I had to trust. As much as the fear lingered, there was no denying that God had brought me to this place, much as I still believed He had when He first called me into ministry those many years ago. It wasn't a call that I took lightly though. I couldn't simply trust that all of the answers were going to be given to me supernaturally — and so I began to read and watch videos in an effort to understand how I could further reconcile what was widely viewed as two irreconcilable entities: the Evangelical church and the transgender community.

By the time Tuesday morning came, I felt like I was somewhat equipped for my conversation with questions about how I could belong. I quickly worked to assure them that I didn't take this lightly — that I understood the concerns about sexual attraction, since I identified as a lesbian-leaning queer woman, and that I was aware of the debate surrounding the bathroom issues. At the same time, I wanted to make it clear that my immediate intent was to grow in my relationship with the Lord as a woman of God. That for most of my life, I wasn't allowed to understand or even embrace the more feminine aspects of my faith, and that with that realization came the understanding that I needed someone to help me embrace this life and learn how to become the best wife and mother I could be.

I pulled into the parking lot of the church offices, applied a little bit more lipstick, and said a quick prayer. I would be lying to say that I wasn't nervous; I was extremely nervous. I hated rejection. The sense of vulnerability reminded me of the days when I would walk through the local shopping centers with the street evangelism team at school to "talk to people about Jesus." As those thoughts began to circle in my head, I found myself smiling. "This is exactly like that," I thought to myself. "Simply share the message that God gave you to share, Ellie, and let God handle it all." This wasn't unlike what I had done before - except that I was being called to speak to believers about God. On top of that, I was meeting with people who guarded the door as to whether or not I could belong in their community. These were people who believed themselves to be the shepherds. Would they see me as a sheep in need of a place to belong, or a wolf that was going to be a threat to the safety of their flock?

Pastor Jeff met me in the front office and led me through a maze of corridors until he ushered me into his office, where Sandy sat waiting. We exchanged pleasantries and before long, I had a captive audience while I shared my story, including how I felt that God was calling me back to church and into community, ending with the question, "is this a community where I could grow and belong?"

"Well, Ellie, I want to thank you for sharing your story," answered Pastor Jeff. "I can't imagine the amount of bravery it took to come in here, not to mention to share everything you've shared with me. I really appreciate that honesty."

"Thank you, Pastor Jeff," I replied. "I'm honestly in a place right now where I just need to know where I can belong. I know, from my own time in ministry, that a church community and church family is essential to the growth of a Christian, and so if I am to grow and thrive as a woman of God..." I trailed off a bit as I watched his facial expression turn to express a sense of sympathy. I shifted, knowing that what was coming wasn't going to be what I wanted to hear.

"Well, Ellie," he began. "I think you also know from your background that where we are as a church means that we see that you taking steps to live as Ellie is sinful. That you are being deceived. I appreciate your theology and your honesty, and I would love to continue to have conversations with you, but as a church, we cannot accept you as a woman."

I nodded silently. I had expected this, so I don't know why there was pain in his answer. "After all," I told myself, "isn't this along the same lines of what you told others who told you that they were gay?"

"We believe that when the Bible says, 'God created them male and female,' that there was no mistake."

"But... isn't that the point? That was when the world was perfect.

That was before sin had entered into the world."

"Yes, but I don't believe that gender is something that God makes mistakes on."

"But is there a possibility?"

"Well, Ellie, there's always the possibility, but... that's not what we believe."

Yes, but. That's where it began to be clearer to me: that no matter what I said in the moment, their training couldn't make space for my identity in their minds.

"Okay."

"Hey, but Ellie?"

"Yes, Pastor Jeff?"

"I'd love to be the person that helps you grow as a Christian. I'd love to talk with you more about where you are and continue this conversation. Would you be up for that?"

I thought for a minute. Perhaps this wasn't the complete rejection and condemnation that I was expecting. Come to think of it, I don't know what I had been expecting.

"Sure," I said, standing up. After a brief hug, we parted ways. The work, as I was to find out, was just beginning.

CHAPTER TWENTY-ONE

Pastor Jeff and I would have a number of further conversations in the months before I finally ended up leaving Fresno. I still consider him a good man, and while we disagreed on whether or not my existence as a transgender woman was a sin, there was one thing that I know he couldn't deny — that my faith was real and authentic. And with that in mind, also came my belief that when the Bible says that "ALL who call upon the name of the Lord shall be saved," (Rom. 10:13) that included me. Follow that up with what Paul wrote just prior to that — "For I am persuaded that neither death nor life, nor angels nor principalities nor powers, nor things present nor things to come, nor height nor depth, nor any other created thing, shall be able to separate us from the love of God which is in Christ Jesus our Lord." (Rom. 8:38-39) There was no denying between either of us that I was a Christian and, as the Evangelicals call it, "saved."

The church upheld their initial request that I do not attend any women's events, and so I began attending the church on the only days that I was allowed to — on Sundays — believing that either way, I was going to be able to worship and learn in a corporate setting, not to mention that my visibility would help demonstrate that I was serious about my desire to grow in my faith and my relationship with God. I truly wanted to be a woman of God, and that wasn't going to happen in a vacuum. The big question remained: Would I ever be able to find a place where I could do that as a woman in the presence of other women? Would I ever find a place that would simply accept me as a woman?

I knew that there were churches in the area that were more progressive. Other churches would accept me and see me fully as a woman. I worked at one such church on Sundays, leading worship for the congregation at a church that was a federation between the United Methodist Church and the United Church of Christ. But my time serving and training in a conservative Evangelical church led me to want to be included in that realm, and I — other than the comfort afforded by the ideology of "we've always done it that way" — couldn't really understand why. And so I set out to see how other churches in the area would respond to the same conversation I had with Sandy that night at the women's event.

"I'm sorry, but we just don't acknowledge that you're a woman," was the response I got most often.

On occasion, I received a direct admonition from the pastor, telling me that I was "living in sin, and blinded to the Truth by my sin." He then went on to tell me how I wasn't going to be welcome into his church until I was willing to repent.

One particular conversation that lasted two hours - with one of the more prominent pastors in town - was very encouraging. I could tell that he genuinely cared and listened intently while I shared my story. He asked questions that showed a lot of thoughtfulness, and I half expected him to surprise me and tell me how I was fully welcome into all aspects of his church.

"Well, Ellie, thank you," he started, after spending two hours talking with me at a local Starbucks. "You have really given me a lot to think about, and I appreciate your bravery. I've never met another trans person before, let alone one who has expressed such a desire to grow in their relationship with God." He paused, shifting his eyes, and I knew. The dreaded answer was coming.

"You see, Ellie," he said, compassion filling his eyes. "I wish I could welcome you into our church with open arms. I wish that I could tell you to take advantage of anything you felt you needed at the church in order to grow in your faith."

I leaned forward, trying to express understanding at knowing what was coming.

"But, you see, we're a Southern Baptist church; one that has planted and maintains a number of churches throughout the area. If we allow you in, then it jeopardizes everything that we're doing. We run the risk of losing our members. Of losing our standing in the denomination. We could lose it all, and so for the greater good, then I'm going to have to say no. I'm really sorry."

I nodded, trying to fight back the tears.

"I don't doubt your salvation. I don't doubt your faith. I'm just really sorry that we're not in a place right now to welcome you in the way that we should be."

"Well, that is one of the reasons why I feel God is calling me to have these conversations."

"And I thank you for that, Ellie. You have a ministry in this."

"Thank you, Pastor."

And with that, we shook hands and went our separate ways.

A ministry? Could this be something that God is calling me to? If it was, I had to come to the realization that in every single conversation that I had up until this point - eight churches in all - every single pastor had told me that I was the first transgender person they had ever met. Perhaps the biggest step was going to be towards visibility. Towards helping people understand that I wasn't some scary pervert that they imagined, just waiting to attack their daughters in the bathroom. No, I was being called to show them that I was a normal Christian woman who loved the Lord. Someone that just happened to be born into the wrong body. Someone who hadn't grown up learning what it meant to be a woman of God, and was in desperate need of someone to help her navigate the world in this new roles she was stepping into: mom, wife, sister, daughter, friend.

As I began to ponder the idea of doing this as some sort of ministry, I also began to wonder if I was alone in this quest to embrace my faith and my identity as a member of the LGBTQ+ community. And, as God does, I was about to find out just how not alone I was.

CHAPTER TWENTY-TWO

Between the meetings I was attending to try and gain business for my new web & graphic design studio and the meetings I was having with various church leaders around the Fresno area, the weeks seemed to go by pretty quickly. Before I knew it, it had gone from September to November. My hair was getting longer, and I was starting to experiment with dresses and more feminine looks, as well as makeup. Things were definitely progressing. I was still attending church regularly on Sunday evenings, and not only did I begin to deepen my faith and relationship with God, but my confidence began to grow as well as I became more and more visible within the Christian community. Even so, it was a lonely place to be - feeling as though I was the only conservative Evangelical Christian who also identified as a queer trans woman. Would I ever find another person who was doing this work? It began to feel as though I was never going to find a place to belong - the LGBTQ+ community, who had been largely persecuted by the faith community didn't understand my connection to faith and God, and the Christian community, who didn't understand how I could reconcile my identity with my faith, continued to tell me that I wasn't fully welcome in their communities, either.

This morning, however, I was leading the congregation at a federated United Methodist and United Church of Christ congregation in worship, and one of our guest speakers was a queer woman. She and I sat and talked for a while at the potluck luncheon following the service, and I began to tell her about my plight and what I had been doing around town with the different pastors.

"You've been doing WHAT?," she exclaimed with disbelief. "I can't believe how brave you are!"

"Well, quite honestly, it is a question that I want answered," I replied. "I can't understand how a church can deny me a place to learn and grow. "

"You know, Ellie, have you ever heard of The Reformation Project?"

My ears perked up. "The Reformation Project?"

"Yeah - they're an organization that is helping train people to do exactly what you're doing."

My mind was swimming. "Wait, Oneida - you're telling me that there are other people doing this work right now?"

"Yes!"

I was speechless. After spending the last few months thinking that I must be alone, and almost resigning myself to the belief that I wouldn't be able to find a community to belong to within the Evangelical Christian church - and trying to make decisions on what pieces of my faith I was going to be able to compromise to fit into some of the more affirming churches - I was just now hearing that I might not be alone in this journey. I rushed home after lunch and googled The Reformation Project - and began reading.

What I found in that afternoon wasn't just a major resource for reconciling my own faith with my identity - complete with background history and exegesis (which for me as a Bible and theology geek, was awesome) - but the organization was just starting to take applications for what they called the TRP Leadership Cohort. The cohort - described as a group of about 50 LGBTQ+ Christians & allies that were spending three months studying at a seminary level the background of how we arrived at the church's stance against LGBTQ+ people and how to work towards inclusion - was a dream come true. I quickly began working on the application, and within a month of just learning about the Reformation Project, I found myself accepted into the Leadership Cohort for the 2019 year.

But it didn't end there. I grew curious as to what other LGBTQ+ Christians there were out there. Searches on Google began producing a number of different people and groups — Kathy Baldock, Austin Hartke, Angel & Nicole Morris, Matthias Roberts, just to name a few. I found myself learning about affirming churches and watching YouTube videos of different presentations. The realization that I wasn't alone anymore was empowering, and I began to wonder what it would be like if I actually found an affirming yet slightly conservative church to attend. Could I find one?

My search took me to the blog of a Southern California pastor who had recently had to take his church through the journey of becoming affirming after his son came out as gay. I read accounts of how he had to figure out, as the pastor of a small church plant, how to love his son and pastor his church through the decision process to become affirming. Of how the congregation, after becoming affirming of LGBTQ+ people, faced a major decrease in attendance. How the pastor had to deal with condemning words from his own congregation as they left. And yet today the church is a small but thriving community of believers that gather each week to worship and draw close to God, and stands as a testament to the work that God is doing within His church towards the inclusion of ALL people.

What is the work that God was calling me towards? By the end of summer 2018, my growing community of friends within the transgender community and the blog I had developed started gaining attention. I was asked to be a guest panelist for a conversation on faith and the LGBTQ+

community at California State University Fresno with two other local pastors and the head of the Center for Gender and Sexuality Studies at the Pacific School of Religion. I spoke locally at business leader meetings and became visible in both local groups and national online groups. I began appearing on podcasts for business, LGBTQ+ issues, and faith. Pretty soon, it was beginning to be hard for me to go places in town without being recognized — and I was really beginning to enjoy the attention.

"Wow, I would have never imagined you as outgoing as you've become," was a comment I heard over and over from friends who knew me pre-transition. Out of sheer curiosity, I took the Myers-Briggs personality quiz and was surprised to see that it had moved from 100% introvert as Darryl to 80% extrovert as Ellie. Things were definitely changing in my life, but not all for the better.

While I was beginning to enjoy the newfound acceptance and attention I was receiving, there was a growing sense of resentment over it from Liz. Gone was the passive uncertainty that Darryl had, and in its place had grown a confident and strong woman with friends and a desire to be social. Things began to unravel in our marriage, and after accepting an invitation to speak at the 2019 Women's March in Fresno as the first transgender woman to speak, the decision was made that we would go our separate ways.

It was a Friday afternoon when I left the house for the last time in

Fresno. Our home. The home that I had expected we would grow old in. I walked into the bedroom we had shared, and Liz was sitting on the bed.

"Well, the car is packed," I said.

"I guess this is it, then."

"Yeah, I guess so."

"Did you say goodbye to the kids?"

"Yes, but I'll go one more time."

I left the room to give each of the children a hug. I told each of them that I loved them, trying to remain strong, but faltering at best.

I walked into the bedroom one more time, pulled the house key and the key to our shared Honda Odyssey off of my keyring, and handed them to her.

"I love you," I said, the tears starting to stream down my face.

She nodded back, unable to say it.

And with that, I walked out of the room. Walked out of the house. And walked away from my marriage and family. My hands were shaking as I put the key in the ignition and started the engine. The sky was dark and overcast as if waiting to break forth with its own flood of tears. I looked back at the house, the tears still streaming down my face. I took a picture of the front of the house through the passenger side window and started the drive towards Southern California where the next chapter of my life awaited.

"Goodbye, Liz."

EPILOGUE

"El-lie Do-te!" The voice pierced the morning tranquility of the backyard from the laptop speakers.

"Hi, Pastor Bill," I replied, briefly unmuting my microphone and taking a sip of coffee.

In the midst of a global pandemic, our small but thriving church has been relegated to weekly online meetings via Zoom. The greetings came one after another as members of the congregation began to log on until five minutes after ten-thirty when the strums of a guitar signaled the opening song and the beginning of the service. I sat back in the white resin patio chair in my parents' backyard and smiled. It's been just over one year since that Friday afternoon when I left my home in Fresno and moved into my parents' home in Southern California. Just over a year since the Sunday morning I walked up to Pastor Bill for the first time at City Church of Long Beach and received that greeting despite having only known him through social media.

This morning, as the sun began to peek through the morning marine layer of clouds revealing a beautiful cerulean sky, a slight breeze blew, sending strands of my long brown hair across my face. I reached up and pulled them slightly back before gathering my hair together and tying it all back in a single ponytail.

In many ways, it's hard to believe that so much change has happened in the span of a year. I was now a single mom, raising a teenager after they moved in with me only a few months after I left the house myself. I completed the coursework for The Reformation Project's Leadership Cohort program, including a four-day summit for the 50 us to gather in Orlando. I was beginning to be seen as a leader within some circles, speaking into and writing about the need for LGBTQ+ inclusion both locally and nationally. EllieGirl is now an active member of both the local and national LGBTQ+ Chambers of Commerce. I serve on an advisory board for a national Facebook group of entrepreneurial women.

It was a Thursday morning after I had moved that I decided I would venture out to Orange County to visit the new campus of the church I once attended two decades earlier. It was the morning of their women's Bible study, and while I half-expected to be turned away, I decided that

I couldn't be left wondering what their response would be if I walked through the door. I found a spot to park my car on the lower level of the two-story parking structure, applied a fresh coat of lipstick, and ventured into the building, Bible in hand.

"Welcome," came a cheery voice from behind a table just inside the door. "Is this your first time here?"

"Um, kind of?" I responded to the young woman a petite blond girl in her mid-twenties. I quickly quantifying my hesitance with, "Well, I used to attend the other campus twenty years ago, and I just moved back into town, so I thought I'd see about visiting this one since it's closer to my house."

"Well, welcome! My name is Amber. Are you here for the women's study?"

"I'd actually like to speak to someone about that, if I could."

"Perhaps I can answer any questions?"

"Oh, if you only knew," I thought to myself. I took a deep breath and proceeded to share a little bit about my identity and how I felt that God was wanting me to find a community that would help me understand and grow in my own life as a woman of God. The more I spoke, though, the more I began to wonder if this was a mistake.

She must have sensed my uncertainty because she stopped me and called over a slightly older woman. She wore a long navy blue skirt with a white blouse and matching accent pieces. Her long brown hair was pulled back so that it flowed neatly down her back. Even in this new enviBobment, there was something familiar about her. My mind began to search the memories as to where I would have known her. Was she here from the other campus?

"This is Shirley," she said to me.

I shook Shirley's outstretched hand, smiling, as Amber continued, "Shirley, this is Ellie. She's visiting us for the first time today."

"Shirley Simons?" I blurted out, as the realization hit me.

"Yes... do I know you?"

"Well, we worked together on that event in San Jose," I reminded her, "though you probably don't recognize me."

Her eyes looked puzzled.

"Back then, I went by a different name. Darryl."

Her eyes widened as the realization began to set in, and then fear.

"Don't worry — I'm not here to cause any trouble," I reassured her. Amber left the two of us to talk and stepped back behind the table as I continued on to share what I had shared with Amber, telling her that I had only recently returned to the faith and was looking for a place where I connect with other women who would help me grow in my relationship with God.

Shirley embraced me. "Of course," she said. "We start out in the main sanctuary," she said, motioning towards the doors behind Amber. "From there, we break out into groups for discussion." Walking me back to Amber, she assigned me to a group and then I went in to find my spot for the opening session.

It was a lovely morning, and as things would go, I was put into a discussion group with Shirley, Amber, a few other women, and Grace, the pastor's wife. We had a lovely discussion, and it was just like being back home. I thanked the women, even stopping to get a hug and photo with Grace, before I walked out of the building and towards my car.

"This is definitely not what I expected," I thought to myself, though I honestly didn't know what I should have expected, considering how I showed up unexpectedly. Encouraged by the morning's reception, I made plans to attend the following evening's Bible study. The reception there was a bit different.

I was met at the door by Shirley's husband, Pastor Bob, who pulled me aside to a corner of the foyer.

"Hello, Pastor Bob," I said, reaching out my hand.

"Hi, um —"

"Ellie," I replied.

"Yes, Ellie. Hello," he said, taking my hand and shaking it.

"I understand from Shirley that you showed up yesterday to the women's study."

"Yes, and it was wonderful."

"Well, I'm sorry, and I wish I was here to greet you yesterday to tell you this, but I'm going to have to ask that you not attend any more women's events here."

My heart dropped. It was the response I had been expecting the morning before, but now? After a successful first visit.

"Ellie, I know that this is a rough time for you," he tried to explain. "But you know where we stand on these issues, so the request shouldn't surprise you."

"It honestly doesn't," I replied, "but I was just hoping…"

"I know. I'm glad that you're here, though. I don't think it was by accident."

"Nor do I," I responded. I honestly didn't think it was an accident, but not in the way that Pastor Bob meant it.

"And hey - you're always welcome to come and visit us for any corporate events."

"Well, I would still love the opportunity to sit and chat with you more," I said.

"Sure, but right now the service is going to start, so…" he trailed off.

"I understand. I need to get in there too."

"Then perhaps next Thursday?"

"Sounds like a plan."

And though we did meet a couple of times since then, the church I once called home had become a strange place; the community that I had once served and had access to had become one where I was kept at a distance. One of the "sinners" that the staff would pray would come to reject everything to conform their life to the box that they taught was "true Christianity."

My experiences weren't all like that, though. In the three years since coming out and beginning hormone treatment, my breasts had continued to develop, and my facial features were softening. My hair had gone from a short bob to a long flowy collection of silky brown strands that stretched past my shoulders. With the change in my appearance came newfound confidence that allowed me to shop as I pleased in most women's sections, though the dressing rooms still held a bit of discomfort for me.

I had begun to allow my natural body movements to take over and reveal themselves, and my femininity really began to show through. I was hired as a part-time ride operator at a local theme park, where most everyone who encountered me identified me as a woman, minus the occasional rude comment from the guests. I've even gotten over my fear of changing in the park's dressing rooms, though I try hard to make sure I keep to myself and not make eye contact. In February 2019, I received my top surgery and woke up to a nice pair of breasts to round out my feminine figure.

Then the world turned upside down, and social distancing became part of our everyday vernacular. Yet in the midst of all of the unknown, God has continued to open doors that allow me to continue sharing my voice and my story far and wide.

Tonight, as I lay in my bed just before drifting off to sleep, I closed my eyes and try to remember the earliest memories of Ellie as I pictured her in the stories I wrote. There was perfection in the world she lived in; a lack of fear that allowed her to belong just as she was, and a freedom that came in not caring what the rest of the world thought.

"Cordelia," I sighed. It's my own personal equivalent to Camelot. It is home. And the freedom I have found in living as Ellie is worth the unknown that lingers ahead as I walk the path towards Cordelia.

A NOTE FROM ELLIE

When I first came out, it was important to me that I be seen as a woman that was attracted to women. I worked hard to try and hide my transgender identity from the world, at times overcompensating with what I thought was feminine mannerisms and expressions. In time, I began to realize that the visibility of others was what helped me understand myself and give me hope. With that in mind, I have learned to step out and embrace my identity as a queer transgender Christian woman. As I read, learn, and listen to stories, I am reminded that for too long in my life I tried to fit into the boxes that would define who I was: Christian. Man of God. Father. Husband. Son. Brother.

We live in a culture that loves definition. We love our labels. Our human nature demands that when we see something, we work as hard as we can to categorize it. It's something that is learned at an early age - we learn through shape sorters about things that fit and things that don't. We learn to color within the lines. We learn to follow directions. And we are taught that God is pleased by that. The problem is, God's very essence transcends anything that we can categorize or understand — as hard as we might try.

"Indescribable, Uncontainable," are the words that become the mantra of a Chris Tomlin song that we used to sing in church on Sundays. We use those words freely to try and talk about God. We know from Moses' encounter with God on Mount Sinai that we cannot even attempt to comprehend God - and that even a glimpse of God's presence is overwhelming. (Exodus 33:18-23) And yet, we still continue to try and put limitations on God:

"No, God couldn't do that. It's not possible that God would allow someone to be born into the wrong gender."

"No, God wouldn't bless a same-sex union. It's just unnatural."

Or, if we were going back further into the past of the church, one might find people limiting God in other ways:

"We could never integrate the black community into our churches, let alone society. It's not God's way."

Our church has a dark history of limiting God - and in doing so, we find ourselves in a dark place where we separate people from God.

Where we erroneously put words into the mouth of God and tell entire groups of people that they are not welcome in the house of God. We build walls and barriers where God meant for them to be broken down. It's why the curtain in the temple was torn in two when Jesus uttered the words, "It is finished." (John 19:30, Matthew 27:51)

It was a rabbi friend of mine who first implored me to take a step back and examine the whole of scripture rather than what the Christian church tends to do. She showed me that throughout Scripture, God is on a never-ending quest to bring about shalom: Wholeness between humanity and God and us with each other. It was a simple revelation; yet one that changed everything for me — and began to give me a new lens in which to view scripture: Is this interpretation helping to restore people to God or each other, or is it helping to divide? Perhaps a unifying paradigm is all that matters, especially when one stops to consider the reality that Jesus was able to boil down everything to two commandments: Love God and love each other. "All of the Law and the Prophets hang on these two commands," He said. (Matthew 22:34-40)

And if that is the quest we are called to — one that calls us to pass every decision and understanding of Scripture through the filter of "does it help me build or destroy shalom on earth?" — then it begs the question of what categorizing and limiting God does.

When I look at the questions surrounding my own label of "queer,"

I have to stop and acknowledge that a good portion of it is a way to deal with my hesitancy to be put back into a category or box. Yes, I do realize that there's an inherent flaw in that type of thinking, but it's also the best I can seem to do, considering that the term "queer" is an overarching label that encompasses anything that is "not straight." My sexual self-identity of queer also points to the realization that everything - sexual and gender identity (which are, in fact, two completely separate identities) - exists on a spectrum. While 99% of who I am identifies as attracted to the feminine, I also have to acknowledge that the night in the bathhouse was not all a horrible experience. There is a 1% part of my identity that could be sexually attracted to a male, but relationally, that is closer to impossible at this point in my life. At the end of the day, the actual label of queer leaves it open with the acknowledgment that this process of self-definition and self-discovery is a journey without a foreseeable end. There are no borders that define my sexuality.

Now, with that being said, I challenge you to take a step back and ask yourself — does your theology and religious beliefs allow for you to help me to grow in my relationship with God and other people, or does it hinder it? Does it place limits on how God can work and who God can call to Himself? Perhaps it's not the LGBTQ+ community. In many ways, my experience with the Church and barriers to being included in the Church has opened my eyes to this injustice on so many different levels. Racism, socioeconomic disparities, and citizenship are just some ways that the Church actively participates in building barriers that prohibit people from connecting to God and connecting to each other.

But where do we go from here? What do we do with this? I would be remiss if I wrote all of this down only to leave it without a message. I mean, what sort of pastor-evangelist would I be if I didn't call you to a decision? Not to worry, though - there's no altar call at the end of this book. No hand to raise, no prayer of salvation to read - not even donations to send in. (Although if you feel led to and want to, I'm not going to complain.) There is, however, a decision that must be made; a challenge that has to be answered - because you can't read a story like mine and not make a decision.

For almost every pastor I've sat with to share my story, too many of them have never met a transgender person, let alone listened to their story. The interesting thing is that the majority of them are pastors of congregations numbering in the thousands. So I sit with them. I share my story. And at the end of the day, they can no longer say that they have not been introduced to the story of a trans person. They can't walk away from the conversation saying that they are indifferent to the journey that has brought me to where I am. And then they are faced with a question that you are faced with now: what do you do with the story I've shared?

There is much more that could be said about my story, just as I am certain that there will be more chapters to come. As much as my story is about transgender and LGBTQ+ rights, at its core is one simple thing: human rights. Are we willing to put aside our ideas and preconceived notions to listen to each other's stories? To wonder about what a person of color might experience as they go about their day doing things that you might take for granted? To listen to the stories of hope that brings a family to risk everything to make a life in America rather than just assuming that their plight is evil and anti-American. It's about putting aside our own selfish comforts in order to sit in the discomfort that comes with hearing the stories of our humanity.

A friend of mine asked me recently what she could do as a cisgender straight woman to be a better ally to the trans community. My answer to her is the same answer I give to you: listen. Listen to our stories, and work for the dignity of all humans. Because we are all created to bear the image of God - each and every person, whether we agree with them or not. Whether we understand them or not. Whether or not they make us comfortable. For me to fight for trans rights while forsaking the rights of my friends who are struggling against racism is just as much an injustice, because it continues the narrative that someone has to be seen as "other." When that status is eliminated, equality will be achieved. And that is shalom. That is God's call to each and every one of us. Peace be with you.

FOR MY TRANS & QUEER FRIENDS

When I first began my journey towards transition, I held on to the stories of my other trans sisters. They were stories of hope; of inspiration. Stories that told me that I wasn't alone. Even then, stories weren't always easy to come by - unless I was looking for articles and stories in which the trans people at the center found themselves in the middle of a legal battle over even existing as who they were meant to be. Add in there the fact that I still had some faint but unbroken ties to Evangelical Christianity, and the sense of failure and loneliness was overwhelming. To be honest, there were many days in there when I wondered if it was worth it. If I should just give into the HIV virus that had taken over my body and hung over my head like a vulture signaling my impending doom.

Yet here I am, not only standing, but having written my first book. As I began this second chapter of my life as a single mom, divorced, and with a world of possibilities in front of me, I began to realize that while the stories that had gotten me here weren't necessarily ones I related to completely, they were stories that resonated and inspired me to become the woman I am today. That's why I decided to put my story in writing - not only to ask the questions that need to be asked of the Church, but to inspire and let you know that you aren't alone.

There's an overwhelming voice that comes from people who claim to be Christian. I've heard it, and I know that I stuck in there longer than many people to finally find a church where I was accepted fully as Ellie. Not just accepted, but celebrated. If nobody has told you this yet, those voices aren't of God. You are loved. You are forgiven. You are precious and a bearer of the image of God. That image echoes deep within you and is calling for you to let it shine. You know what it is - and it is beautiful.

When Adam and Eve ate of the fruit in the garden, immediately Satan turned on them, and shame set in. They became ashamed of who they were. Who they were didn't change - what changed is that they felt shame. They felt disconnected from God. The voice of condemnation began to shout down at them to tell them that they were not worthy of God's love. So they hid.

There will be voices along the way who tell you that you should be ashamed of who you are. That God will never accept you as you are. Those voices are not of God. I cannot state that clearer than this.

I don't know where you are in your story, and I know that my story may not mirror your own journey. That's okay. Your story is unique, and it paints a glorious picture of the infinite glory of God. Yet in your unique path, remember - you're not alone. May my story bring that reality to light for you.

                        Blessings,

                        Ellie

RESOURCES

As I noted at the beginning of this book, I did not set out to write a book arguing the theology behind who I am. Rather, I felt like it was important to share my story in a way that would be read from beginning to end with the hope that if my readers desired to learn more about the next steps in affirming the LGBTQ+ people in their lives, they could take steps to do so. After all, there are so many people who have dedicated so much of their lives into the research and theology behind affirming theology, and their voices deserve to be heard; their work seen.

With that in mind, I have compiled a list of several of the resources, groups, and information that has helped me in my journey to embrace my own faith and my identity as a queer transgender Christian woman. While this isn't an exhaustive list, I do hope that it will provide a jumping off point for you to learn more and ask the questions that need answering in today's church.

BOOKS

- *Ancient Laws and Contemporary Controversies: The Need for Inclusive Biblical Interpretation* by Dr. Cheryl Anderson
- *Walking the Bridgeless Canyon* by Kathy Baldock
- *Shameless: A Sexual Reformation* by Nadia Bolz-Weber
- *Bible, Gender, Sexuality: Reframing the Church's Debate on Same-Sex Relationships* by James V. Brownson
- *Refocusing My Family* & *Unashamed: A Coming-Out Guide for LGBTQ Christians* by Amber Cantorna
- *Searching for Sunday: Loving, Leaving, and Finding the Church* by Rachel Held Evans
- *Bad Theology Kills: Undoing Toxic Belief & Reclaiming Your Spiritual Authority* by Kevin Garcia
- *Transforming: The Bible & The Lives of Transgender Christians* by Austin Hartke
- *Building a Bridge: How the Catholic Church and the LGBT Community Can Enter into a Relationship of Respect, Compassion, and Sensitivity* by James Martin, SJ
- *Beyond Shame: Creating a Healthy Sex Life on Your Own Terms* by Matthias Roberts
- *OutLove: A Queer Christian Survival Story* by Julie Rodgers
- *God and the Gay Christian* by Matthew Vines

WEBSITES

- *AIDS Healthcare Foundation* (hivcare.org)
- *Beloved Arise* (belovedarise.org)
- *The Christian Closet* (thechristiancloset.com)
- *Church Clarity* (churchclarity.org)
- *Freed Hearts* (freedhearts.org)

- *Free Mom Hugs* (freemomhugs.org)
- *The One Frontier* (theonefrontier.com)
- *Pastor Ellie Dote* (pastorellie.com)
- *PFLAG* (pflag.org)
- *Q Christian Fellowship* (qchristian.org)
- *The Reformation Project* (reformationproject.org)
- *The Trevor Project* (thetrevorproject.org)
- *Transmission Ministry Collective* (transmissionministry.com)

PODCASTS

- *The Bible For Normal People with Pete Enns*
- *The Confessional with Nadia Bolz-Weber*
- *New Abbey Church*
- *Queerology with Matthias Roberts*
- *Lavender Mafia with Jess Garcia & Jack Bates*
- *For the Love Podcast with Jen Hatmaker*

MOVIES

- *The Trans List* (HBOMax)
- *Pray Away* (Netflix)

OTHER RESOURCES

- *OurBible* (iPhone & Android app)
- *Angel & Nicole* (YouTube Channel)

ACKNOWLEDGMENTS

It would be crazy to think that my story was experienced in a bubble. That the things learned along the way - allowing me to share these insights with you - came from many conversations and learning communities which have shaped my faith and my transition over the past several years. I would also be remiss to acknowledge the people of faith along the way who have walked with me through all of the various stages of my faith - from my Catholic upbringing to my time in the Calvary Chapel network to my studies at BIOLA University and into my time as a pastor at Friends Community Church in Fresno, California, leading to my time as the graphic designer at Fremont Community Church in Fremont, California. I look back at my entire life, and lest you think otherwise, every step has been a blessing from God. It hasn't been without pain - but the pain results in growth. Each step is an opportunity to grow - and I hope that has been evident in my writing.

So, with that, here is a (far from exhaustive) list of people I am extremely grateful to in the process of this book and my story becoming a reality.

- **For my children:** I am so proud of you all. I know that I wasn't easy to live with as Dad, and that I put you all through a lot while your mother and I worked through my diagnosis with AIDS and the following year as I began to heal and come out at the same time. Even though we're not the family I once envisioned those twenty years ago, the love I have for each of you has never changed. I love you.

- **For Kayla & Michelle:** Thank you for being the first ones to see me and welcome me as Ellie in public. Your friendship that first day made me realize that I didn't have to walk this journey alone. I wouldn't be where I am today without that first experience with you, so thank you.

- **For Christy and Pastor Shane:** Thank you for being faithful to the call that God has put on your life. I appreciated the time you invested in me to make sure that I knew I was loved by God, and for having so many of those early theological conversations when I was just trying to come to terms with who I was both as Ellie and as a Christian.

- **For the communities at Woven Fresno, City Church of Long Beach, & New Abbey:** Thank you for showing me what it means to be fully welcomed as I am into the family of God.

- **For Jen H.:** You have remained one of my best friends through everything, from the early days of navigating Christianity to urging me to write for the Crossbearer's newsletter to our days at Biola and now through this change. Thank you for remaining with me through it all.

- **For Stephanie:** There isn't much that I can say here that wouldn't be a major understatement of what you mean to me. I am so grateful for your presence in my life and for the encouragement you gave me to finish this project. I love you.

- **For Anna:** When I first put this project together, I had no clue what I was doing. And yet God knew that I needed to meet you at just the right time to help give me the tools I needed to make this book that much better for my readers.

- **For Liz:** You are a complete God thing in my life. I don't know how else to describe the amazing friend you have become since we met in that Facebook group. You truly are a kindred spirit; the Diana to my Anne.

- **For Theresa:** Your courage inspires me. Thank you for trusting me and for walking this journey with me.

- **For my friends and family at The Reformation Project, Austin Hartke, and Kathy Baldock:** Thank you for helping me see not only that I am loved by God, but for helping me find my calling in sharing that message with the world, and giving me so many tools and resources to do so.

- **For Valerie & Cid:** Thank you for encouraging me not only to write this book, but for helping me see my inherit self-worth in the midst of the changes my life has brought.

- **For Jeanne & Richard C.:** I was only a child when we lost Richard to AIDS, and I never forgot that. When I was first diagnosed, your story was what immediately came to mind, and it is your story that reminds me of the power of storytelling.

- **For Renee A.:** Thank you for inspiring me with your writings and for showing me - and the world - the power of storytelling.

- **For Mrs. Michalski & Ms. Zieg:** Your encouragement and love for the English language helped me to become the writer I am today. Thank you for believing in me.

- **For my parents:** I know that some of the things in this book may have even been a shock to you. I have put you through so much and I know that my transition has not been easy. Yet you accepted me - welcomed me - back into your home, and recognize me as your daughter. I am lucky.

- **For my sister & brother-in-law:** What can I say except I love you both. It's been so wonderful to build my relationship with you as your sister. Thank you for accepting and embracing me.

- **For "Liz":** I know that the past years have been painful for you. I know this wasn't easy. But I also recognize that I wouldn't be where I am today without you, and for that I am grateful. I honestly can say that I love you, even if our paths have diverged.

www.ingramcontent.com/pod-product-compliance
Lightning Source LLC
Chambersburg PA
CBHW011802090426
42811CB00037B/2356/J